D1289440

Easy BUNDLE

KETO DESSERTS

Two Years of Low Carb Desserts,
Snacks and Fat Bombs

Elizabeth Jane

INTRODUCTION

Two years ago, a reader requested 'a year of fat bombs'. "Well, I normally fix meals to last me at most four serving or days. I'd plan to have a fat bomb every day.

That's 365 days divided by a recipe that makes at least a weeks' worth, so 52 recipes? That's ideal. Are there 52 fat bomb recipes anywhere?

Perfection in my mind would be a seasonally adjusted book where you would split the recipes into four seasons. To allow for not always sweet but savory recipes utilizing available produce and lots of fat. How's that for a crazy idea?"

And so 'A Year of Fat Bombs' was created, 52 sweet and savory recipes seasonally themed using ingredients available for that time of the year. The book went on to be a huge success. Recently I set about creating 'the second book in this series, 'A Year of Easy Keto Desserts". Again, it was a huge success.

Another reader requested a compilation of both books, giving them 105 easy desserts and fat bombs in one book, and so we launched 'Two Years of Keto Desserts & Fat Bombs'.

I hope this dessert book becomes a staple in your kitchen and that it brings a little joy and that it brings you joy in allowing you to create and enjoy some guilt-free treats.

I would love to hear any feedback from you. Also, if you have any questions regarding any of the recipes at all, please do not hesitate to email me at:

Elizabeth@ketojane.com

You May Also Like

HOMEMADE KETO SOUP

http://ketojane.com/soup

KETO BREAD BAKERS COOKBOOK

http://ketojane.com/bread

The answer to your keto dinnertime dilemma. Easy keto and low-carb friendly soups and stews to satisfy your soul, all with *less than 5g of net carbs!*

The Keto Bread Bakers cookbook contains all the bread that you thought you had to give up.

Everyone loves bread! And if you're on a special diet and miss bread, then this book is for you! Paleo, low carb, gluten free, keto, wheat free, but still the same great tastes.

Free Easy Keto Meals

I guarantee you will love all the recipes in the Keto Pasta & Noodles cookbook, but there are some times when you want to throw something together in 2-3 minutes.

These free keto sauces can be made in minutes and thrown on just about any keto dish to change them from 'everyday' to yummy! If you are in a real hurry, smother them on some store-bought noodles and you have an immediate delicious keto meal.

From rubs to marinades and butters, there are simple and delicious recipes to complement whatever you are making.

Visit http://www.ketojane.com/sauces to download your free copy.

CONTENTS

15

FALL

COOKIES

FUDGE/SAVORY BITES

DONUTS/SCONES

DESSERT BEVERAGES

COLD TREATS

FAT BOMBS

42

WINTER

COOKIES

SAVORY BITES & CHOCOLATE

BROWNIES, PIES & LOAF BREAD

COLD TREATS

FAT BOMBS

71

SPRING

SAVORY BITES & CHOCOLATES

BROWNIES & CAKE

COLD TREATS

FAT BOMBS

98

SUMMER

HOW THIS
Book Works

This cookbook contains helpful baking tips to help you get the best results possible. There are also serving suggestions included to give you an idea about what each of these recipes pair well with.

You will also notice there are five symbols on the top right-hand side of each recipe. A key to these symbols is set out below:

PREPARATION TIME:

 Time required to prepare the recipe. This does not include cooking time.

COOKING TIME:

 Time required to cook the recipe. This does not include the preparation time.

SERVINGS:

 How many servings each recipe requires. This can be adjusted. For example, by doubling the quantity of all of the ingredients, you can make twice as many servings.

YOUR GUIDE TO MAKING DELICIOUS
Keto Desserts

To help you get started, I put together a quick guide on how you can get the most out of baking and how you can make whipping up keto desserts fun and delicious.

Here are some tips to help you make the most delicious keto dessert you've tried yet!

 # 1   **FOCUS ON QUALITY:** Quality is really going to matter here. I made sure to keep these recipes simple enough where you can actually taste that vanilla extract or taste the hints of shredded coconut. You want to be able to taste these flavors, so focus on a getting a high-quality pure vanilla extract and high-quality baking spices to really bring the flavors out.

 # 2 **GET THE NATURALLY FLAVORED STEVIA:** You will find I use stevia in many of these recipes for a couple of reasons. For one, it keeps the carb count down, and number two, you can get some flavored stevia options (my personal favorite is the vanilla cream) that adds a nice touch to your baking recipes. Just be sure to stick to the ones that are naturally flavored VS artificial.

 # 3 **FOCUS ON THE FAT:** Us keto-dieters are used to adding lots of fat into our diet, and when it comes to these dessert recipes, I have used a lot of coconut oil and butter, so be sure to stock up on these! You will be using them liberally in many of the recipes.

 # 4 **MAKE IT PALEO:** Looking to make your recipes Paleo-friendly? Try swapping out the dairy by using coconut milk instead of milk and coconut oil instead of butter.

 # 5 **HAVE FUN:** Not everyone loves to bake, so I tried to make these recipes simple and not very time-consuming so we could bring some fun back to baking keto-friendly desserts. Have fun with it! After all, the end result will be a delicious treat you can enjoy without the guilt.

A NOTE ON SWEETENERS &
Specialty Ingredients

As a way to add variation to these dessert recipes, you will find a variety of low-carb sweeteners used. However, feel free to swap one for the other. For example, if you prefer stevia over erythritol, use stevia! If you can't find monk fruit, you can try using Swerve instead. Feel free to be creative, and use whatever low-carb sweetener you prefer in each recipe.

The same goes for certain specialty ingredients like aluminum-free baking powder. For the purpose of making many of these recipes Paleo friendly in addition to keto-approved, you will find that a recipe calls for aluminum and gluten-free baking powder. Feel free to use regular baking powder if you are unable to find the aluminum and gluten-free version.

Many recipes also call for liquid vanilla stevia, but you can feel free to use regular liquid stevia, or a flavor of your choice!

You will also come across some recipes that call for ghee. If you are unable to find ghee, feel free to use butter instead.

These recipes are designed to be delicious and bring the fun back into baking keto desserts, so feel free to adjust the ingredients to your taste and preference!

FALL

PEANUT BUTTER THUMBPRINT *Cookies*

Difficulty Level: 2	20 minutes (plus cooling time)	8-10 minutes	x16 (1 cookie per serving) $$

GF DF

INGREDIENTS:

- 2 cups unsweetened peanut butter (use almond butter for a paleo version)
- 2 eggs
- 2 tsp. liquid stevia
- 1 tsp. pure vanilla extract
- 1 tsp. gluten- and aluminum-free baking powder

Filling:

- ½ cup coconut oil
- ½ cup of dark unsweetened chocolate chips

Nutritional Information:

Carbs: 8g	**Fat:** 27g
Fiber: 3g	**Protein:** 8g
Net Carbs: 5g	**Calories:** 298

DIRECTIONS:

1. Preheat the oven to 350 degrees F and line a baking sheet with parchment paper.
2. Add the peanut butter and eggs to a mixing bowl and stir.
3. Add in the remaining ingredients and mix well.
4. Drop by 1-inch rounds onto the parchment-lined baking sheet.
5. Using your thumb, press into the center of each cookie.
6. Bake for 8-10 minutes or until the edges begin to brown.
7. While the cookies are baking, add the coconut oil and dark chocolate chips to a stockpot over low to medium heat and stir until melted.
8. Once the cookies are done, scoop about 1 teaspoon of the chocolate mixture into the center of each cookie.
9. Allow the chocolate center to harden and enjoy.

Preparation Instructions:

You can also use sugar-free jam in the center of these cookies if you aren't a fan of chocolate. Add the jam before the cookies go into the oven.

Serving Suggestions:

Serve with a glass of unsweetened almond milk.

THE ULTIMATE FALL SPICE KETO CHOCOLATE CHIP *Cookies*

Difficulty Level: 2	10 minutes (plus cooling time)	14-16 minutes	x12 (1 cookie per serving) $$

GF

INGREDIENTS:

- 2 cups finely ground almond flour
- 2 eggs
- ½ cup butter, melted (use coconut oil for a paleo version)
- ½ cup raw cacao nibs
- 3 Tbsp. monk fruit sweetener
- 1 tsp. gluten- and aluminum-free baking powder
- 1 tsp. pumpkin pie spice
- ½ tsp. ground cinnamon
- 1 tsp. pure vanilla extract
- ½ tsp. sea salt

DIRECTIONS:

1. Preheat the oven to 350 degrees F and line a baking sheet with parchment paper.
2. Add the melted butter, vanilla, and eggs to a mixing bowl and whisk.
3. Add all of the dry ingredients to a mixing bowl minus the cacao nibs and mix well.
4. Whisk the wet mixture into the dry and whisk until no lumps remain.
5. Fold in the cacao nibs.
6. Drop by the rounded tablespoon, making 12 large cookies onto the parchment-lined baking sheet and bake for 14-16 minutes or until the edges begin to brown.
7. Cool and enjoy!

Preparation Instructions:

You can also use unsweetened dark chocolate chips if you are unable to find raw cacao nibs.

Serving Suggestions:

Serve with a glass of unsweetened almond milk.

Nutritional Information:

Carbs: 6g

Fiber: 2g

Net Carbs: 4g

Fat: 14g

Protein: 3g

Calories: 158

NUTMEG & CINNAMON *Cookies*

WITH NO-CARB VANILLA ICING

Difficulty Level: 1 | 10 minutes | 14-16 minutes | x14 (1 cookie per serving) $$

GF

INGREDIENTS:

- 2 ½ cups finely ground almond flour
- 2 eggs
- ½ cup butter, melted (use coconut oil for a paleo version)
- 3 Tbsp. monk fruit sweetener (use pure maple syrup for a paleo version)
- 1 tsp. gluten- and aluminum-free baking powder
- 1 tsp. ground nutmeg
- 1 tsp. ground cinnamon
- 1 tsp. pure vanilla extract
- ½ tsp. sea salt

Frosting:

- 1 cup heavy whipping cream (use unsweetened coconut cream for a paleo version)
- ¼ cup Swerve (use pure maple syrup for a paleo version)
- 2 tsp. pure vanilla extract

Nutritional Information:	
Carbs: 6g	Fat: 13g
Fiber: 1g	Protein: 2g
Net Carbs: 5g	Calories: 130

DIRECTIONS:

1. Preheat the oven to 350 degrees F and line a baking sheet with parchment paper.
2. Add the melted butter, vanilla and eggs to a mixing bowl and whisk.
3. Add all dry ingredients except cacao nibs to a mixing bowl and mix well.
4. Whisk the wet mixture into the dry and whisk until no lumps remain.
5. Drop by the rounded tablespoon, making 14 cookies onto the parchment-lined baking sheet and bake for 14-16 minutes or until the edges begin to brown.
6. While the cookies are baking, make the vanilla frosting by adding all ingredients to a high-speed blender, or add to a mixing bowl and, using a hand mixer, whip until soft peaks form.
7. Allow the cookies to cool, and then top with a dollop of the vanilla frosting.

Preparation Instructions:

You can add a tablespoon of raw, unsweetened cocoa to make these cookies even more decadent.

Serving Suggestions:

Serve with a glass of unsweetened almond milk.

PUMPKIN CHEESECAKE
Fat Bombs

INGREDIENTS:

- 1 cup whipped cream cheese
- 2 Tbsp. ghee
- ¼ cup pure pumpkin puree
- 1 tsp. pumpkin pie spice
- 1 tsp. pure vanilla extract
- 10 drops liquid vanilla stevia

Difficulty Level: 1 | 15 minutes (plus chilling time) | 0 minutes | x8 (1 fat bomb per serving) $$

GF

DIRECTIONS:

1. Add the whipped cream cheese, ghee, and pumpkin puree to a food processor or blender and blend until the mixture is mixed and "fluffy."
2. Add the pumpkin pie spice, vanilla extract, and stevia and whip again.
3. Pour the mixture into silicone baking molds. Alternatively, line mini muffin tins with muffin liners, and scoop about 1 tablespoon of the mixture into each mold or muffin liner.
4. Freeze for about 1 hour before serving, and store leftovers in the freezer.

Preparation Instructions:

You can use regular butter instead of ghee if preferred.

Serving Suggestions:

Serve with a mug of hot coffee or tea for a delicious after-dinner treat.

Nutritional Information:

Carbs: 5g

Fiber: 0g

Net Carbs: 5g

Fat: 13g

Protein: 2g

Calories: 133

SEA SALT & CARAMEL FUDGE SAVORY *Bites*

Difficulty Level: 1	15 minutes (plus chilling time)	0 minutes	x10 (1 bite per serving) $$

GF DF V

INGREDIENTS:

- 1 cup coconut oil
- 10 drops vanilla liquid stevia
- ¼ cup raw unsweetened cocoa powder
- 1 tsp. pure vanilla extract
- 1 tsp. sugar-free caramel extract
- 1 pinch sea salt

DIRECTIONS:

1. Line mini cupcake tins with cupcake liners and add the coconut oil and stevia to a mixing bowl and whip with a handheld mixer.
2. Add the cocoa powder, vanilla, caramel extract, and salt.
3. Pour into the lined muffin tins and freeze for about 20 minutes or until set.
4. Enjoy and store leftovers covered in the freezer.

Preparation Instructions:

You can also use silicone cupcake molds to make these.

Serving Suggestions:

Serve with a glass of unsweetened almond milk.

Nutritional Information:	
Carbs: 1g	**Fat:** 22g
Fiber: 1g	**Protein:** 0g
Net Carbs: 0g	**Calories:** 194

PEANUT BUTTER *Fudge*

Difficulty Level: 1 | 15 minutes (plus chilling time) | 0 minutes | x10 (1 piece per serving) $$

GF DF V

INGREDIENTS:

- 1 cup coconut oil
- 10 drops liquid stevia
- ½ cup unsweetened peanut butter (use almond butter for a paleo version)
- 1 tsp. pure vanilla extract
- 1 pinch sea salt

DIRECTIONS:

1. Line a baking sheet with parchment paper and add the coconut oil and stevia to a mixing bowl and whip with a handheld mixer.
2. Add the peanut butter, vanilla, and salt.
3. Scoop the mixture onto the lined baking sheet and flatten to about 1-inch thick.
4. Freeze for about 20 minutes or until set and cut into small squares.
5. Store leftovers covered in the freezer.

Nutritional Information:

Carbs: 3g	**Fat:** 28g
Fiber: 1g	**Protein:** 2g
Net Carbs: 2g	**Calories:** 261

Preparation Instructions:

You can also make these into mini fudge bites using mini cupcake silicone molds.

Serving Suggestions:

Serve with a cup of tea or coffee.

CHOCOLATE
Truffles

Difficulty Level: 2	10 minutes (plus chilling time)	5 minutes	18 (1 truffle per serving) $$

GF

INGREDIENTS:

- 1 cup unsweetened dark chocolate chips
- 4 Tbsp. butter
- ¾ cup heavy cream
- ¼ cup Swerve
- ½ tsp. pure vanilla extract
- ½ cup raw unsweetened cocoa powder for coating

DIRECTIONS:

1. Add the chocolate chips and butter to a stockpot over low heat. Stir until melted.
2. Mix in the Swerve and vanilla extract.
3. Remove from heat and stir in the heavy cream.
4. Refrigerate the mixture for at least 4 hours.
5. Once chilled, scoop the hardened chocolate mixture out with a small cookie scoop and drop onto a parchment-lined baking sheet.
6. Sprinkle with the cocoa powder and refrigerate until ready to enjoy.

Preparation Instructions:

You can use 1 teaspoon of stevia in place of Swerve if desired.

Serving Suggestions:

Serve with a cup of tea or coffee.

Nutritional Information:	
Carbs: 8g	**Fat:** 12g
Fiber: 3g	**Protein:** 2g
Net Carbs: 5g	**Calories:** 135

CINNAMON & CLOVE *Donuts*

Difficulty Level: 2 | 20 minutes | 0 minutes | x6 (1 donut per serving) $$

GF

INGREDIENTS:

- 1 cup finely ground almond flour
- 2 eggs
- ¼ cup unsalted butter, melted (use melted ghee for a paleo version)
- ¼ cup heavy cream (use full-fat unsweetened coconut milk for a paleo version)
- 1 tsp. ground cinnamon
- ¼ tsp. ground cloves
- 2 tsp. aluminum and gluten-free baking powder
- 1 tsp. pure vanilla extract
- 2 tsp. liquid stevia
- Coconut oil for greasing

Cinnamon & Clove Coating:

- ½ cup melted coconut oil
- 2 Tbsp. monk fruit in the raw sweetener
- 1 Tbsp. ground cinnamon
- ¼ tsp. ground cloves

Nutritional Information:

Carbs: 4g	**Fat:** 31g
Fiber: 2g	**Protein:** 3g
Net Carbs: 2g	**Calories:** 299

DIRECTIONS:

1. Preheat the oven to 350 degrees F and grease a donut pan
2. Make the donut mixture by adding all the dry ingredients to a large mixing bowl and stir.
3. Whisk the eggs, melted butter, heavy cream, vanilla, and stevia in a separate bowl, and then whisk slowly into the dry mixture. Whisk until no lumps remain.
4. Pour the mixture into the pregreased donut pan and bake for 20-25 minutes.
5. While the donuts are baking, make the cinnamon and clove coating by whisking together monk fruit, cinnamon, and ground cloves in a large mixing bowl. Set aside.
6. Once the donuts are done, allow them to cool and then melt the coconut oil in a large mixing bowl. Dunk each donut into the melted oil, covering both sides.
7. Immediately sprinkle with the cinnamon and clove mixture. Also sprinkle on some powdered stevia if desired.

Preparation Instructions:

If you aren't a fan of cloves, you can use cinnamon, increasing the amount to 1¼ teaspoon in the donut mixture and 1¼ tablespoon in the coating mixture.

Serving Suggestions:

Serve with a dollop of cream cheese if desired.

MAPLE CINNAMON *Scones*

INGREDIENTS:

- 1¼ cups finely ground almond flour
- ¼ cup unsweetened coconut milk
- 1 egg
- ¼ cup monk fruit sweetener
- 1 tsp. gluten- and aluminum-free baking powder
- 2 Tbsp. butter, melted (use melted coconut oil for a paleo option)
- 1 tsp. pure vanilla extract
- 1 tsp. ground cinnamon
- 1 tsp. sugar-free maple extract (use 1 Tbsp. pure maple syrup for a paleo version)
- ½ tsp. sea salt

Difficulty Level: 2 | 15 minutes | 20 minutes | x6 (1 scone per serving) $$

DIRECTIONS:

1. Preheat the oven to 350 degrees F and line a baking sheet with parchment paper.
2. Add the dry ingredients to a large mixing bowl and mix well.
3. Add the coconut milk, the egg, melted butter, vanilla extract, and maple extract. Mix well.
4. Form the dough into a large round and place on the baking sheet and flatten to about 1-inch thick.
5. Cut into 6 wedges and bake for about 20 minutes or until the edges begin to brown.
6. Cool and enjoy!

Preparation Instructions:

You can add fresh fruit like raspberries to the batter if desired.

Serving Suggestions:

Serve with whipped cream cheese if desired.

Nutritional Information:

Carbs: 3g

Fiber: 2g

Net Carbs: 1g

Fat: 10g

Protein: 3g

Calories: 105

SPICED HOT
Chocolate

Difficulty Level: 1	5 minutes	5 minutes	x1 (approx. ½ cup) $

GF DF V

INGREDIENTS:

- ½ cup full-fat unsweetened coconut milk
- 1 Tbsp. raw unsweetened cocoa powder
- ¼ tsp. ground cinnamon
- ⅛ tsp. ground nutmeg
- ⅛ tsp. ground cloves
- 1 tsp. pure. Vanilla extract
- 1 drop vanilla cream liquid stevia

DIRECTIONS:

1. Add all the ingredients to a stockpot over low or medium heat and whisk until warmed through.
2. Pour into your favorite mug and enjoy!

Preparation Instructions:

Add a pinch of pumpkin spice if desired.

Serving Suggestions:

Serve with a dollop of unsweetened whipped cream if desired.

Nutritional Information:	
Carbs: 10g	**Fat:** 30g
Fiber: 5g	**Protein:** 4g
Net Carbs: 5g	**Calories:** 292

Cold Treats
PUMPKIN-SPICED CACAO *Mousse*

Difficulty Level: 1 | 15 minutes (plus chilling time) | 0 minutes | x4 (approx. ¼ cup per serving) $$

GF DF V P

INGREDIENTS:

- 2 cups of canned unsweetened full-fat coconut milk (place can in the refrigerator overnight)
- ½ cup pure pumpkin puree
- 2 Tbsp. raw unsweetened cacao powder
- ½ tsp. pumpkin pie spice
- 10 drops liquid vanilla stevia

DIRECTIONS:

1. Add the coconut cream to a blender or food processor, and whip for about 2 minutes until creamy.
2. Add remaining ingredients and blend until combined.
3. Scoop the mixture into 4 small serving glasses or bowls, and chill for at least 1 hour before serving.

Serving Suggestions:

Serve with an extra sprinkle of pumpkin pie spice if desired.

Nutritional Information:	
Carbs: 5g	**Fat:** 8g
Fiber: 2g	**Protein:** 1g
Net Carbs: 3g	**Calories:** 87

COCONUT CREAM
PUMPKIN *Pie Milkshake*

Difficulty Level: 1 | 10 minutes | 0 minutes | x2 (approx. a ½ cup per serving) $$

GF DF V P

DIRECTIONS:

1. Add all ingredients to a high-speed blender and blend until smooth.
2. Enjoy right away.

Preparation Instructions:

For canned coconut milk, blend the contents of the can first to combine the coconut milk and cream evenly.

Serving Suggestions:

If you are not avoiding dairy, you can also make this recipe using heavy cream.

INGREDIENTS:

- 1 cup full-fat unsweetened coconut milk
- ¼ cup pure pumpkin puree
- ¼ tsp. pumpkin pie spice
- 1 tsp. pure vanilla extract

Nutritional Information:

Carbs: 8g   **Fat:** 29g

Fiber: 3g   **Protein:** 3g

Net Carbs: 5g **Calories:** 288

MAPLE WALNUT
Whipped Cream

Difficulty Level: 2 | 20 minutes (plus chilling time) | 0 minutes | x8 (approx. ¼ cup per serving) $$

GF

INGREDIENTS:

- 2 cups heavy whipping cream
- 2 Tbsp. ghee
- 2 tsp. sugar-free maple extract
- 1 tsp. pure vanilla extract
- 1 cup chopped walnuts
- 10 drops liquid vanilla stevia
- ½ tsp. guar gum

DIRECTIONS:

1. Place a large mixing bowl in the fridge to chill for about 20 minutes.
2. Remove the chilled bowl and add the heavy whipping cream. Whip using a handheld blender until stiff peaks form.
3. Add the remaining ingredients minus the walnuts and guar gum. Whip until combined.
4. Fold the chopped walnuts and guar gum in gently and store in an airtight container in the freezer overnight or for at least 8 hours before enjoying.

Preparation Instructions:

You can make this ahead of time, store in the fridge, and then whip one more time before serving.

Serving Suggestions:

Serve with a bowl of your favorite keto ice cream.

Nutritional Information:	
Carbs: 3g	**Fat:** 24g
Fiber: 1g	**Protein:** 4g
Net Carbs: 2g	**Calories:** 230

ALMOND DELIGHTS

Serves : 12
Preparation time : 10 minutes
Cooking time : None
Freezing time : 2 hours

ADDITIONAL TIP

I suggest melting butter over a double boiler because direct melting can scald and burn the butter, hence ruining the taste. Try adding in some chopped almonds for some added texture

INGREDIENTS:

- 18 ounces grass-fed butter
- 2 ounces heavy cream
- ⅔ cup cocoa powder
- ½ cup granulated Stevia
- 4 tablespoons almond butter
- 1 teaspoon vanilla extract

DIRECTIONS:

1. Melt the butter over a double boiler.

2. Add in the rest of the ingredients and mix well.

3. Place into your favorite molds and freeze for 2 hours.

NUTRITION FACTS (PER SERVING)

Calories: 350   Fat: 38g   Protein: 2g   Total Carbohydrates: 4g   Dietary Fiber: 2g   Net Carbohydrates: 0g

SALTED
CARAMEL CONES

Serves : 12   Preparation time : 5 minutes   Cooking time : None   Freezing time : 2 hours

INGREDIENTS:

- ⅓ cup coconut oil
- ⅓ cup grass-fed butter
- 2 tablespoons heavy whipping cream
- 2 tablespoons sour cream
- 1 tablespoon caramel sugar
- 1 teaspoon sea salt
- Stevia to taste

DIRECTIONS:

1. Soften the butter and coconut oil.

2. Mix all the ingredients to form a batter.

3. Pour into a cone or triangle shaped molds. Freeze until they set.

4. Sprinkle with a little more salt on top and enjoy!

5. Store in the fridge.

ADDITIONAL TIP

Don't use regular table salt. Use a more coarse salt like kosher or sea salt, which gives the best texture and flavor.

NUTRITION FACTS (PER SERVING)

Calories: 100   Fat: 12g   Protein: 0g   Total Carbohydrates: 1g   Dietary Fiber: 0g   Net Carbohydrates: 1g

MINI
CINNAMON BUNS

Serves : 12   Preparation time : 5 minutes   Cooking time : None   Freezing time : 2 hours

INGREDIENTS:

- 8 ounces cream cheese
- ½ cup grass-fed butter
- 4 tablespoons coconut oil
- 1 teaspoon vanilla extract
- ¼ teaspoon ground cinnamon
- ⅛ teaspoon ground nutmeg
- Stevia to taste

DIRECTIONS:

1. Soften the butter and coconut oil. Mix in the cream cheese.

2. Add in the rest of the ingredients and mix until homogenous.

3. Pour into silicone molds and freeze until set.

ADDITIONAL TIP
Drizzle a little sugar-free caramel syrup on top.

NUTRITION FACTS (PER SERVING)

Calories: 165   Fat: 18g   Protein: 1g   Total Carbohydrates: 1g   Dietary Fiber: 0g   Net Carbohydrates: 1g

CHAI BITES

Serves : 12   Preparation time : 5 minutes   Cooking time : None   Freezing time : 2 hours

INGREDIENTS:

- 1 cup cream cheese
- 1 cup coconut oil
- 2 ounces grass-fed butter
- 2 teaspoons ground ginger
- 2 teaspoons ground cardamom
- 1 teaspoon ground nutmeg
- 1 teaspoon ground cloves
- 1 teaspoon Darjeeling black tea
- 1 teaspoon vanilla extract
- Stevia to taste

DIRECTIONS:

1. Melt the butter and coconut oil in a saucepan and add the black tea. Wait for it to color the mixture.

2. Add in cream cheese and remove from heat. Stir well.

3. Add in all the spices and stir to make a batter.

4. Pour into silicon molds and freeze until they set.

5. Enjoy with some actual tea or in the evenings in place of tea.

6. Store in the refrigerator.

NUTRITION FACTS (PER SERVING)

Calories: 178   Fat: 19g   Protein: 1g   Total Carbohydrates: 1g   Dietary Fiber: 0g   Net Carbohydrates: 1g

MAPLE & PECAN BARS

Serves : 12
Preparation time : 10 minutes
Cooking time : 25 minutes
Freezing time : None

ADDITIONAL TIP

Since they are baked, they can be stored in an airtight jar at room temperature for up to a week.

INGREDIENTS:

- 2 cups chopped pecans
- 1 cup almond meal
- ½ cup sugar-free chocolate chips
- ½ cup flaxseed meal
- ½ cup coconut oil (heat slightly to become liquid)
- ½ cup sugar-free maple syrup
- 20-25 drops Stevia

DIRECTIONS:

1. Spread the pecans in a baking dish and bake at 350 degrees until aromatic (will usually take from 6 to 8 minutes).

2. In the meanwhile, sift together all the dry ingredients.

3. Add the roasted pecans to the mix and mix well.

4. Add the maple syrup and coconut oil and stir to make a thick, sticky mixture.

5. Pour in a bread pan lined with parchment paper.

6. Bake for about 18 minutes at 350°F or until the top has browned.

7. Slice and enjoy!

NUTRITION FACTS (PER SERVING)

Calories: 302   Fat: 30g   Protein: 5g   Total Carbohydrates: 6g   Dietary Fiber: 4g   Net Carbohydrates: 2g

PUMPKIN
PIE FAT BOMBS

Serves : 12   Preparation time : 35 minutes   Cooking time : 5 minutes   Freezing time : 3 hours

INGREDIENTS:

- ⅓ cup pumpkin puree
- ⅓ cup almond butter
- ¼ cup almond oil
- 3 ounces sugar-free dark chocolate
- 2 tablespoons coconut oil
- 1 ½ teaspoon pumpkin pie spice mix
- Stevia to taste

DIRECTIONS:

1. Melt dark chocolate and almond oil over a double boiler.

2. Layer the bottom of 12 muffin cups with this mixture and freeze until the crust has set.

3. Meanwhile, combine the rest of the ingredients in a saucepan and put on low heat.

4. Heat until softened and mix well.

5. Pour this over the initial chocolate mixture and chill for at least 1 hour.

ADDITIONAL TIP
Use pumpkin puree without any added ingredients.

NUTRITION FACTS (PER SERVING)

Calories: 124   Fat: 13g   Protein: 3g   Total Carbohydrates: 3g   Dietary Fiber: 1g   Net Carbohydrates: 2g

CHOCO-PB EXPLOSIONS

Serves : 12
Preparation time : 12 minutes
Cooking time : 20 minutes
Freezing time : None

INGREDIENTS:

- 2 cups almond flour
- ⅓ cup crunchy peanut butter
- ¼ cup coconut oil (heat gently so it is liquid)
- 4 ounce dark chocolate bar (sugar free)
- 3 tablespoon sugar-free maple syrup
- 1 tablespoon vanilla extract
- 1 ¼ teaspoon baking powder
- A pinch of salt

DIRECTIONS:

1. In a large bowl, whisk together all the wet ingredients. The mixture will be light brown.

2. In another bowl, mix all the dry ingredients except the chocolate.

3. Now sift dry ingredients into the wet ingredients while continuing to mix. You want the batter to be smooth and not lumpy.

4. A crumbly mixture will form. Form this crumbly mixture into a ball and wrap it in cling film. Refrigerate for about an hour.

5. While the ball is in the fridge, cut up chocolate into small 1-inch pieces.

6. Take out dough from the fridge and make small balls. Place a piece of chocolate in the middle of each ball.

7. Line on a baking tray.

8. Bake for about 18 minutes at 350°F.

9. Sprinkle with some ground cinnamon, cool and enjoy

NUTRITION FACTS (PER SERVING)

Calories: 148   Fat: 13g   Protein: 4g   Total Carbohydrates: 4g   Dietary Fiber: 2g   Net Carbohydrates: 2g

COCOA-COATED BACON BOMBS

Serves : 12
Preparation time : 10 minutes
Cooking time : 50 minutes
Freezing time : None

ADDITIONAL TIP

You can also fry the bacon instead of baking.

INGREDIENTS:

- 12 bacon slices
- 1 tablespoon sugar-free maple syrup
- Granulated Stevia to taste

FOR THE COATING:

- ¼ cup chopped pecans
- 4 tablespoons dark cocoa powder
- 15-20 drops Stevia

DIRECTIONS:

1. Lay the bacon slices on a baking tray and rub with maple syrup and Stevia. Flip the slices and do the same with the other side.

2. Bake for 10-15 minutes at 275°F (until crispy).

3. When done, drain the bacon grease.

4. Mix the bacon grease, cocoa powder and Stevia to form a batter.

5. Dip the bacon slices in the batter, roll in chopped pecans and allow to air dry until the chocolate hardens.

NUTRITION FACTS (PER SERVING)

Calories: 157   Fat: 11g Protein: 10g   Total Carbohydrates: 1g   Dietary Fiber: 0g   Net Carbohydrates: 1g

NUTTY NOUGATS

Serves   : 12
Preparation time : 5 minutes
Cooking time   : 5 minutes
Freezing time   : 1 hour

ADDITIONAL TIP

Don't like the nuts listed? Use whatever nuts you like.

INGREDIENTS:

- 4 ounces cocoa butter
- 2 ounces chopped macadamia nuts
- 2 ounces chopped walnuts
- 2 ounces chopped pecans
- 1 cup heavy cream
- 2 tablespoons cocoa powder
- Stevia to taste

DIRECTIONS:

1. Melt the cocoa butter over a double boiler. Gradually stir in cocoa powder and Stevia.

2. Mix well. Remove from heat.

3. Whisk in heavy cream and fold all the nuts in.

4. Pour into molds and refrigerate until set.

NUTRITION FACTS (PER SERVING)

Calories: 367   Fat: 28g   Protein: 3g   Total Carbohydrates: 3g   Dietary Fiber: 0g   Net Carbohydrates: 3g

FRIED
FRESCO CHEESE

Serves	: 12
Preparation time	: 2 minutes
Cooking time	: 5-7 minutes
Freezing time	: None

ADDITIONAL TIP

You can also add various spices to enhance the flavor.

INGREDIENTS:

- 2 pounds queso fresco
- 2 tablespoons coconut oil
- 1 tablespoon olive oil
- 1 tablespoon chopped basil

DIRECTIONS:

1. Heat together coconut and olive oil in a pan.
2. Cut the cheese into small cubes.
3. Fry in oil. Make sure to fry all sides until brown.
4. Sprinkle with fresh basil and enjoy!

NUTRITION FACTS (PER SERVING)

Calories: 243   Fat: 19g   Protein: 16g   Total Carbohydrates: 0g   Dietary Fiber: 0g   Net Carbohydrates: 0g

APPLE ROUNDS

Serves : 12   Preparation time : 5 minutes   Cooking time : 5 minutes   Freezing time : 3 hours

INGREDIENTS:

- 2 medium-sized apples
- 5 ounces heavy cream
- ½ cup grass-fed butter
- 2 tablespoons coconut oil
- 1 teaspoon ground cinnamon
- Stevia to taste
- A pinch of salt

DIRECTIONS:

1. Thinly slice the apples.

2. Melt the coconut oil in a pan and add in the apples and cinnamon. Mix well to coat the apples.

3. Cook until they become tender. Softly mash them with your spoon.

4. Remove from heat and fold in rest of the ingredients.

5. Pour into candy molds (preferably apple shaped) and freeze for about 3 hours.

6. Store in the refrigerator.

ADDITIONAL TIP

Apples are relatively high in carbohydrates, so use these as an occasional treat

NUTRITION FACTS (PER SERVING)

Calories: 168   Fat: 12g   Protein: 0g   Total Carbohydrates: 10g   Dietary Fiber: 2g   Net Carbohydrates: 8g

CREAM CHEESE CLOUDS

Serves : 5 minutes
Preparation time : None
Cooking time : 12
Freezing time : hour

ADDITIONAL TIP

You can also different flavored extracts (e.g. orange, peppermint etc.) to make a variety of flavors.

INGREDIENTS:

- ½ cup grass-fed butter
- 8 ounces cream cheese
- ½ teaspoon vanilla extract
- Stevia to taste

DIRECTIONS:

1. Whisk everything together using an electric beater until frothy.

2. Drop spoonfuls onto a tray and freeze until set.

NUTRITION FACTS (PER SERVING)

Calories: 134   Fat: 14g   Protein: 1g   Total Carbohydrates: 1g   Dietary Fiber: 1g   Net Carbohydrates: 0g

SPICY PUMPKIN FAT BOMBS

Serves : 12
Preparation time : 10 minutes
Cooking time : 6 minutes
Freezing time : Overnight

ADDITIONAL TIP

A really fun thing that you can do is that you can add a few of these bombs (or the pre-frozen mixture) to a food processor and blend with some coconut or regular dairy milk to get an instant pumpkin smoothie. Add some instant coffee for a quick latte

INGREDIENTS:

- ½ cup diced pumpkin
- 3 tablespoons coconut butter
- 1 ½ tablespoons coconut oil
- ¼ teaspoon ground ginger
- ¼ teaspoon ground nutmeg
- ¼ teaspoon ground cinnamon
- ⅛ teaspoon ground cloves
- Stevia to taste

DIRECTIONS:

1. Melt the coconut oil and add it to the coconut butter. Add in Stevia and whisk until smooth.

2. Add the diced pumpkin and the spices to a food processor and pulse to roughly chop them up into very small pieces.

3. Mix the two together and stir well.

4. Make into small balls and line on a piece of parchment paper.

5. Place in the fridge and allow to set.

NUTRITION FACTS (PER SERVING)

Calories: 99   Fat: 10g   Protein: 2g   Total Carbohydrates: 1g   Dietary Fiber: 0g   Net Carbohydrates: 1g

WINTER

MEGA-CHOCOLATE CHUNK CHOCOLATE
Chip Cookies

INGREDIENTS:

- 2 cups finely ground almond flour
- 2 eggs
- ½ cup butter, melted (use coconut oil for a paleo version)
- ½ cup unsweetened dark chocolate chunks
- 3 Tbsp. monk fruit sweetener
- 1 tsp. gluten- and aluminum-free baking powder
- 1 tsp. pure vanilla extract
- ½ tsp. sea salt

Difficulty Level: 1 | 15 minutes | 14-16 minutes | x16 (1 cookie per serving) $$

GF

DIRECTIONS:

1. Preheat the oven to 350 degrees F, and line a baking sheet with parchment paper.
2. Add the eggs, melted butter, and vanilla to a large bowl and whisk.
3. Add the rest of the ingredients and mix well.
4. Drop by the rounded tablespoon onto the parchment lined baking sheet and bake for 14-16 minutes or until the edges begin to brown.

Preparation Instructions:

You can also use 1 teaspoon of stevia in place of the monk fruit if preferred.

Serving Suggestions:

Serve with a cup of unsweetened almond milk.

Nutritional Information:

Carbs: 3g

Fiber: 1g

Net Carbs: 2g

Fat: 12g

Protein: 3g

Calories: 130

CHEWY BROWNIE MINI *Cookies*

Difficulty Level: 1 | 10 minutes (plus chilling time) | 0 minutes | x20 (1 cookie each) $$

GF

INGREDIENTS:

- ⅓ cup coconut flour, sifted
- ¼ cup raw unsweetened cocoa powder
- ½ cup raw cacao nibs
- 1 cup butter, melted (use ghee for a paleo version)
- 2 eggs
- ½ cup Swerve
- 1 tsp. pure vanilla extract
- ½ tsp. sea salt

Preparation Instructions:

You can use 1 teaspoon of stevia powder in place of the Swerve if preferred.

Serving Suggestions:

Serve with a glass of unsweetened almond or coconut milk.

DIRECTIONS:

1. Preheat the oven to 350 degrees F and line a baking sheet with parchment paper.
2. Add the melted butter, eggs, and vanilla to a large mixing bowl and whisk.
3. Add the dry ingredients and mix until no lumps remain.
4. Scoop the dough by the rounded teaspoon and bake for 10-14 minutes or until the edges begin to get crispy and the center of the cookie begins to set.

Nutritional Information:

Carbs: 4g	**Fat:** 15g
Fiber: 3g	**Protein:** 1g
Net Carbs: 1g	**Calories:** 153

KETO GINGERBREAD
Cookies

Difficulty Level: 2	15 minutes (plus chilling time)	10-12 minutes	x18 (1 cookie each) $$

GF

DIRECTIONS:

1. Preheat the oven to 350 degrees F and line a baking sheet with parchment paper.
2. Add the almond flour, spices, baking powder, and sea salt to a large mixing bowl and whisk well.
3. Cream the butter by adding it to a large mixing bowl and whipping with a handheld mixer. Add the monk fruit sweetener, molasses, and vanilla and whip again.
4. Add the eggs one at a time mixing again until combined.
5. Pour the almond flour mixture in slowly and mix with the handheld mixer until combined well.
6. Drop by rounded tablespoons onto the lined baking sheet and press down gently to flatten. For an added holiday touch use your favorite holiday-inspired cookie cutter!
7. Bake 10-12 minutes or until the edges begin to brown.
8. Allow to cool before enjoying.

INGREDIENTS:

- 2 cups finely ground almond flour
- 2 eggs
- 1 cup butter, melted (use coconut or ghee for a paleo version)
- ⅓ cup monk fruit sweetener
- 1 tsp. baking powder
- 1 tsp. ground cinnamon
- ½ tsp. ground ginger
- ¼ tsp. ground nutmeg
- ⅛ tsp. ground cloves
- 1 tsp. pure vanilla extract
- ⅛ tsp. sea salt
- 1½ tsp. blackstrap molasses

Preparation Instructions:

To cream the butter, if you don't have a handheld mixer, you can add the butter to a food processor or high-speed blender.

Serving Suggestions:

Serve with a glass of unsweetened almond or coconut milk.

Nutritional Information:

Carbs: 5g	**Fat:** 12g
Fiber: 0g	**Protein:** 1g
Net Carbs: 5g	**Calories:** 118

SNOWFLAKE CHRISTMAS SPICE
Sugar Cookies

Difficulty Level: 2	15 minutes (plus chilling time)	7-10 minutes	x16 (1 cookie each) $$

GF

INGREDIENTS:

- 1 cup almond flour
- 2 Tbsp. coconut flour (sifted)
- ½ tsp. baking powder
- ¼ tsp. ground nutmeg
- ⅛ tsp. ground cloves
- ½ cup butter (use coconut oil or ghee for a paleo version)
- ¼ cup erythritol
- 1 tsp. pure vanilla extract
- ⅛ tsp. salt

Preparation Instructions:

To cream the butter, you can also use a handheld mixer.

Serving Suggestions:

Serve with a glass of unsweetened almond or coconut milk.

Nutritional Information:	
Carbs: 5g	**Fat:** 7g
Fiber: 1g	**Protein:** 1g
Net Carbs: 4g	**Calories:** 69

DIRECTIONS:

1. Preheat the oven to 350 degrees F and line a baking sheet with parchment paper.
2. Cream the butter by adding it to a food processor. Blend with the vanilla until fluffy.
3. Add the remaining dry ingredients to a large mixing bowl and stir to combine.
4. Pour dry mixture into the blender or food processor slowly and blend until combined.
5. Place the dough in the fridge for about 15 minutes.
6. Once chilled, place the dough onto the parchment-lined baking sheet and roll to about 1-inch thick on a greased surface. Alternatively, you could line another large baking sheet with parchment paper and roll the dough out on the sheet.
7. Using a snowflake cookie cutter, cut into snowflake shapes and place on the parchment-lined baking sheet.
8. Bake for 7-10 minutes or until the edges begin to brown.
9. Cool completely before enjoying!

THE ULTIMATE LOW-CARB APPLE PIE *Savory Bites*

INGREDIENTS:

- 1 cup raw cashews
- ½ cup unsweetened coconut butter
- 1 red apple, skin removed, finely chopped
- ½ tsp. ground cinnamon
- ¼ tsp. ground nutmeg
- 1 tsp. pure vanilla extract
- ¼ tsp. sea salt

Preparation Instructions:

You can also use a Granny Smith apple if preferred.

Serving Suggestions:

Serve with a cup of hot tea of coffee.

Nutritional Information:	
Carbs: 8g	**Fat:** 13g
Fiber: 3g	**Protein:** 2g
Net Carbs: 5g	**Calories:** 150

Difficulty Level: 1 | 10 minutes (plus chilling time) | 0 minutes | x16 (1 bite per serving) $$

GF DF V P

DIRECTIONS:

1. Add the cashews and coconut butter to a food processor, and process until the mixture comes together.
2. Add in the remaining ingredients and blend until mixed well.
3. Place the mixture in the fridge for 10 minutes.
4. While the mixture is chilling, line a baking sheet with parchment paper.
5. Roll the chilled dough into 16 rounds and place on the lined baking sheet.
6. Refrigerate for at least 1 hour before serving.
7. Store leftovers covered in the fridge.

VALENTINE'S DAY CHOCOLATE RASPBERRY
Fat Bombs

INGREDIENTS:

- 1 cup whipped cream cheese
- 2 Tbsp. ghee
- ¼ cup unsweetened dark chocolate chips
- ¼ cup frozen raspberries
- 1 tsp. pure vanilla extract
- 10 drops liquid vanilla stevia

Difficulty Level: 1 | 10 minutes (plus chilling time) | 0 minutes | x12 (1 fat bomb each) $$

Preparation Instructions:

You can use butter instead of ghee if preferred.

Serving Suggestions:

Serve with a mug of hot coffee for a tasty Valentine's Day dessert.

DIRECTIONS:

1. Add the whipped cream cheese, ghee, and raspberries to a food processor or blender and blend until the mixture is mixed and "fluffy."
2. Add the vanilla extract and stevia and whip again.
3. Fold in the dark chocolate chips and then pour the mixture into silicone baking molds, filling all the way.
4. Freeze for about 1 hour before serving and store leftovers in the freezer.

Nutritional Information:	
Carbs: 2g	**Fat:** 12g
Fiber: 1g	**Protein:** 2g
Net Carbs: 1g	**Calories:** 122

DARK CHOCOLATE PEPPERMINT *Bark*

INGREDIENTS:

- ½ cup coconut oil
- ¼ cup full-fat unsweetened coconut milk
- ¼ cup raw unsweetened cocoa powder
- ½ tsp. pure peppermint extract
- ² tsp. pure vanilla extract
- ¹⁰ drops liquid vanilla stevia
- ¼ tsp. sea salt

Difficulty Level: 2 | **10 minutes** (plus chilling time) | **5 minutes** | **x12** (1 piece per serving) **$$**

GF DF V P

Preparation Instructions:

You can also add ¼ cup raw cocoa nibs to the chocolate mixture for added crunch.

Serving Suggestions:

Serve with a glass of unsweetened almond milk.

Nutritional Information:

Carbs: 1g   **Fat:** 11g
Fiber: 1g   **Protein:** 1g
Net Carbs: 0g   **Calories:** 94

DIRECTIONS:

1. Line a baking pan with parchment paper.
2. Add the coconut oil to a saucepan over low to medium heat and warm until melted.
3. Whisk in the coconut milk, cocoa powder, peppermint, and vanilla extract.
4. Add the stevia, and sea salt.
5. Pour the mixture into the lined baking pan and freeze for 15-20 minutes or until set.
6. Once set, slice into 12 pieces and store leftovers covered in the fridge or freezer for future use.

BLONDIES

Difficulty Level: 2 | 15 minutes | 20-25 minutes | x8 (1 blondie per serving) $$

GF DF V P

INGREDIENTS:

- 2 cups finely ground almond flour
- 2 eggs
- ½ cup coconut oil, melted
- 1 tsp. powdered stevia
- 1 tsp. pure vanilla extract
- ½ cup of unsweetened dark chocolate chips
- 1 tsp. gluten- and aluminum-free baking powder

Preparation Instructions:

If you cannot find unsweetened chocolate chips, you can also use raw cocoa nibs.

Serving Suggestions:

Serve with a dollop of unsweetened whipped cream if desired.

DIRECTIONS:

1. Preheat the oven to 350 degrees F, and line a 9x13-inch baking pan with parchment paper.
2. Add eggs to a mixing bowl and whisk.
3. Mix in the coconut oil, vanilla extract, and stevia. Mix well.
4. Fold in the almond flour, baking powder, and dark chocolate chips.
5. Pour the mixture into the lined baking pan and bake for 20-25 minutes or until the edges begin to brown.
6. Cool, and then slice into 8 squares.

Nutritional Information:	
Carbs: 6g	**Fat:** 26g
Fiber: 3g	**Protein:** 5g
Net Carbs: 3g	**Calories:** 275

EGGNOG *Brownies*

Difficulty Level: 2 | 15 minutes | 20-25 minutes | x8 (1 brownie per serving) $$

INGREDIENTS:

- 2 cups finely ground almond flour
- 2 eggs
- ½ cup coconut oil, melted
- ¼ cup raw unsweetened cocoa powder
- ¼ cup unsweetened dark chocolate chips
- 1 tsp. powdered stevia
- 1 tsp. pure vanilla extract
- 1 tsp. ground cinnamon
- ½ tsp. ground nutmeg
- 1 tsp. gluten- and aluminum-free baking powder
- ⅛ tsp. sea salt
- 2 Tbsp. water

DIRECTIONS:

1. Preheat the oven to 350 degrees F, and line a 9x13-inch baking pan with parchment paper.
2. Add the eggs to a mixing bowl and whisk.
3. Mix in the coconut oil, vanilla extract, and stevia. Mix well.
4. Add the almond flour, baking powder, cocoa powder, cinnamon, nutmeg, sea salt, and water. Mix well.
5. Fold in the chocolate chips, pour the mixture into the lined baking pan and bake for 20-25 minutes or until a toothpick inserted into the center comes out clean.
6. Cool, and then slice into 8 squares.

Preparation Instructions:

If you are not avoiding dairy, you can use butter instead of coconut oil if preferred.

Serving Suggestions:

Serve with a dollop of unsweetened whipped cream if desired.

Nutritional Information:

Carbs: 6g

Fiber: 3g

Net Carbs: 3g

Fat: 23g

Protein: 4g

Calories: 233

CHRISTMAS-INSPIRED PECAN PIE *Savory Bites*

INGREDIENTS:

- 1 cup raw pecans
- ½ cup shredded unsweetened coconut
- 2 Tbsp. coconut butter
- 1 tsp. pure vanilla extract
- 10 drops liquid vanilla stevia
- 1 tsp. ground cinnamon
- ¼ tsp. allspice
- ¼ cup raw cacao nibs

Difficulty Level: 2 | 10 minutes (plus chilling time) | 0 minutes | x12 (1 bite per serving) $$

GF DF P

DIRECTIONS:

1. Add the pecans and shredded coconut to a high-speed blender or food processor and blend until combined well.
2. Add the coconut butter, vanilla, stevia, cinnamon, and allspice and blend again.
3. Pour the mixture into a mixing bowl and fold in the cacao nibs.
4. Refrigerate to chill for 15 minutes.
5. Once chilled, roll into bite-sized rounds.
6. Store leftovers covered in the fridge.

Preparation Instructions:

You can use raw walnuts or cashews in place of the pecans if preferred.

Serving Suggestions:

Serve with a mug of keto eggnog for a holiday treat.

Nutritional Information:

Carbs: 8g

Fiber: 6g

Net Carbs: 2g

Fat: 30g

Protein: 3g

Calories: 298

COFFEE CAKE LOAF WITH NO-CARB *Vanilla Icing*

Difficulty Level: 2	20 minutes	20-30 minutes	x8 (1 slice per serving) $$

GF

INGREDIENTS:

- 2½ cups almond flour
- ½ cup brewed coffee, chilled
- 3 eggs
- ½ cup ghee, melted
- 1 tsp. powdered stevia
- 1 tsp. ground cinnamon
- 1 tsp. pure vanilla extract

No-Carb Vanilla Icing:

- 1 cup whipped cream cheese
- ¼ cup heavy whipping cream
- 1 tsp. liquid vanilla cream stevia
- 1 tsp. pure vanilla extract

Preparation Instructions:

To make this paleo-friendly, try using almond-based cream cheese and full-fat unsweetened coconut cream.

Serving Suggestions:

Serve with a mug of keto hot chocolate or a hot cup of coffee.

DIRECTIONS:

1. Line a loaf pan with parchment paper and preheat the oven to 325 degrees F.
2. Add the eggs to a mixing bowl and whisk.
3. Add the ghee, vanilla extract, and coffee and whisk again.
4. Add the dry ingredients and whisk until no lumps remain.
5. Bake for 20-30 minutes or until a toothpick inserted into the center comes out clean.
6. While the loaf is baking, make the frosting by adding the ingredients to a food processor, and whip until creamy.
7. Once the loaf is cool, top with the frosting, slice into 8 even pieces and enjoy!

Nutritional Information:

Carbs: 6g	**Fat:** 19g
Fiber: 1g	**Protein:** 6g
Net Carbs: 5g	**Calories:** 218

HOLIDAY SPICED CHOCOLATE CUPCAKES WITH *Buttercream Frosting*

INGREDIENTS:

- 1 cup coconut flour
- ½ cup unsweetened cocoa powder
- 1 tsp. powdered stevia
- 3 eggs
- 1 cup half and half
- ½ cup butter, melted
- 2 tsp. pure vanilla extract
- 2 tsp. baking powder
- 1 tsp. ground cinnamon
- ½ tsp. ground nutmeg

Buttercream Frosting

- ½ cup butter
- ½ cup whipped cream cheese
- 2 tsp. Pure vanilla extract
- 2 drops of liquid vanilla stevia (optional)

Difficulty Level: 1	15 minutes	18-20 minutes	x16 (1 cupcake per serving) $$

Cooking tip:

Coconut flour is very absorbent, so the batter will be thicker than traditional cake batter. Instead of pouring the mixture into the muffin tin, scoop with a spoon and gently press down to flatten.

DIRECTIONS:

1. Start by preheating the oven to 350 degrees F and lining a muffin tin with liners.
2. Add all of the dry ingredients to one bowl and mix well.
3. In a separate bowl, whisk the eggs. Mix in the half and half, melted butter, and pure vanilla extract.
4. Pour the wet mixture into the dry and stir until well-combined and until no clumps remain.
5. Scoop the cupcake batter into the lined muffin tins, filling ¾ of the way.
6. Bake at 350 for 18-20 minutes.
7. Cool completely before frosting with the buttercream frosting.

Buttercream Frosting Directions:

1. Add all the frosting ingredients to a large bowl and cream using a hand-held mixture. Alternatively, use a food processor and whip until well combined.
2. Transfer the mixture to a piping bag, and frost each cupcake once completely cool.

Nutritional Information:

Carbs: 12g   **Fat:** 18g

Fiber: 7g   **Protein:** 4g

Net Carbs: 5g   **Calories:** 226

CHOCOLATE PEPPERMINT
Christmas Loaf

Difficulty Level: 2	20 minutes	20-30 minutes	x8 (1 slice per serving) $$

 GF

INGREDIENTS:

- 2½ cups almond flour
- ¼ cup raw unsweetened cocoa powder
- ½ cup unsweetened almond milk
- 3 eggs
- ½ cup butter, melted (use ghee for a paleo version)
- 1 tsp. powdered stevia
- 1 tsp. pure peppermint extract
- ¼ cup unsweetened dark chocolate chips

Preparation Instructions:

Feel free to add some additional holiday flair by including 1 teaspoon ground nutmeg if desired.

Serving Suggestions:

Serve with a mug of tea or hot coffee.

DIRECTIONS:

1. Line a loaf pan with parchment paper and preheat the oven to 325 degrees F.
2. Add the eggs to mixing bowl and whisk.
3. Add the butter, peppermint, and almond milk, and whisk again.
4. Add all the dry ingredients and whisk until no lumps remain.
5. Bake for 20-30 minutes or until a toothpick inserted into the center comes out clean.
6. Allow the loaf to cool for 10 minutes. Slice and enjoy!

Nutritional Information:

Carbs: 6g	**Fat:** 22g
Fiber: 3g	**Protein:** 6g
Net Carbs: 3g	**Calories:** 234

WALNUT PARFAIT WITH CINNAMON
Streusel

INGREDIENTS:

- 1 cup full-fat unsweetened Greek yogurt (use full-fat unsweetened coconut milk yogurt for a paleo version)
- ¼ cup chopped walnuts
- 1 tsp. pure vanilla extract
- ½ tsp. ground cinnamon

Cinnamon Streusel:

- 3 Tbsp. coconut oil
- ½ cup chopped walnuts
- 1 tsp. Swerve sweetener
- 2 tsp. ground cinnamon

Difficulty Level: 1 | 10 minutes (plus chilling time) | 0 minutes | x4 (approx. ¼ cup per serving) $$

GF

DIRECTIONS:

1. Add yogurt to the base of a serving bowl and stir in the vanilla and cinnamon.
2. Top with the chopped walnuts and set aside.
3. Make the cinnamon streusel by adding all the ingredients to a mixing bowl and mix well.
4. Add the cinnamon streusel on top of the yogurt bowl and enjoy!

Preparation Instructions:

You can make this parfait using pecans if preferred.

Serving Suggestions:

Enjoy with a dollop of unsweetened whipped cream if desired.

Nutritional Information:

Carbs: 8g

Fiber: 3g

Net Carbs: 5g

Fat: 30g

Protein: 9g

Calories: 313

BREAKFAST
BACON BOMBS

Serves : 12   Preparation time : 10 minutes   Cooking time : 15 minutes   Freezing time : 1 hour

INGREDIENTS:

- 8 bacon slices
- 4 eggs
- ⅔ cup grass-fed butter
- 2 tablespoons full-fat keto-friendly mayonnaise
- 1 tablespoon chopped cilantro
- ¼ teaspoon cayenne pepper
- Salt and pepper to taste

DIRECTIONS:

1. Hard boil the eggs.
2. While the eggs are boiling, fry the bacon until crispy. Reserve the bacon grease.
3. When done, peel the eggs and mash them with a fork. Mix in butter, mayonnaise and seasonings.
4. Crumble the bacon into small pieces and mix into the main mixture.
5. Refrigerate for at least an hour.
6. Form into small balls and return to the fridge.

ADDITIONAL TIP
Customize the seasonings to your liking.

NUTRITION FACTS (PER SERVING)

Calories: 185   Fat: 18g   Protein: 5g   Total Carbohydrates: 0g   Dietary Fiber: 0g   Net Carbohydrates: 0g

CREAMY
COCONUT FUDGE

Serves	: 12
Preparation time	: 20 minutes
Cooking time	: None
Freezing time	: 2 hours

ADDITIONAL TIP

You can also make these into balls but squares are much more convenient.

INGREDIENTS:

- 2 cups coconut oil
- ½ cup coconut cream
- ½ cup dark cocoa powder
- ¼ cup chopped almonds
- ¼ cup shredded coconut
- 1 teaspoon almond extract
- A pinch of salt
- Stevia to taste

DIRECTIONS:

1. Pour coconut cream and coconut oil into a large bowl and whisk using an electric beater. Stop when the mixture becomes smooth and glossy.

2. Slowly begin to add cocoa powder while continuing to mix. Make sure that there are no lumps.

3. Add in the rest of the ingredients.

4. Pour into a bread pan lined with parchment paper and freeze until set.

5. Cut into squares and enjoy!

NUTRITION FACTS (PER SERVING)

Calories: 172   Fat: 20g Protein: 0g   Total Carbohydrates: 1g   Dietary Fiber: 1g   Net Carbohydrates: 0g

NUTMEG NOUGATS

Serves : 12
Preparation time : 10 minutes
Cooking time : 5 minutes
Freezing time : 30 minutes

ADDITIONAL TIP

You can also coat them in cocoa powder instead.

INGREDIENTS:

- 1 cup cashew butter
- 1 cup heavy cream
- 1 cup shredded coconut
- 1 teaspoon vanilla extract
- ½ teaspoon ground nutmeg
- Stevia to taste

DIRECTIONS:

1. Melt the cashew butter over a double boiler.
2. Stir in dairy cream, vanilla extract, nutmeg and Stevia.
3. Remove from heat and allow to cool down a little.
4. Place in the refrigerator for at least half an hour.
5. Remove from the fridge and shape into small balls.
6. Coat with shredded coconut and chill for 2 hours. Then serve.

NUTRITION FACTS (PER SERVING)

Calories: 341   Fat: 34g   Protein: 3g   Total Carbohydrates: 13g   Dietary Fiber: 8g   Net Carbohydrates: 5g

COCOA BROWNIES

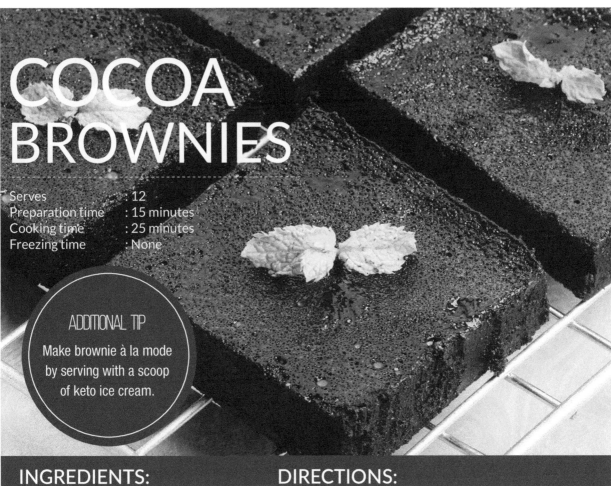

Serves : 12
Preparation time : 15 minutes
Cooking time : 25 minutes
Freezing time : None

ADDITIONAL TIP

Make brownie à la mode
by serving with a scoop
of keto ice cream.

INGREDIENTS:

- 1 egg
- ⅓ cup heavy cream
- ¾ cup almond butter
- ¼ cup cocoa powder
- 2 tablespoons grass-fed butter
- 2 teaspoon vanilla extract
- ¼ teaspoon baking powder
- A pinch of salt

DIRECTIONS:

1. Break the egg and whisk until smooth.

2. Add in all the wet ingredients and mix well.

3. Mix all the dry ingredients and sift them into the wet ingredients to make a batter.

4. Pour into a greased baking pan and bake for 25 minutes at 350°F or until a toothpick inserted in the middle comes out clean.

5. Cool, slice and serve.

NUTRITION FACTS (PER SERVING)

Calories: 184   Fat: 20g   Protein: 1g   Total Carbohydrates: 1g   Dietary Fiber: 0g   Net Carbohydrates: 1g

ORANGE OODLES

Serves	: 12
Preparation time	: 10 minutes
Cooking time	: None
Freezing time	: 2 hours

ADDITIONAL TIP

These are a versatile recipe. Try a variety of garnishes / additions. Some suggestions: toasted chopped nuts, shredded coconut, (more) cocoa powder

INGREDIENTS:

- 10 ounces coconut oil
- 4 tablespoons cocoa powder
- ¼ teaspoon blood orange extract
- Stevia to taste

DIRECTIONS:

1. Melt half the coconut oil over a double boiler and add in Stevia and orange extract.

2. Pour this mixture into candy molds, filling halfway.

3. Refrigerate until set.

4. In the meantime, melt the remaining coconut oil and stir in the cocoa powder and some Stevia. Make sure that there are no lumps.

5. Pour this into the molds, filling them up.

6. Return to your fridge and chill until completely set.

NUTRITION FACTS (PER SERVING)

Calories: 188   Fat: 21g   Protein: 1g   Total Carbohydrates: 1g   Dietary Fiber: 0g   Net Carbohydrates: 1g

MINI
MINTY HAPPINESS

Serves : 12   Preparation time : 45 minutes   Cooking time : None   Freezing time : 2 hours

INGREDIENTS:

- 1 ½ cups coconut oil
- 1 ¼ cups sunflower seed butter
- 1 cup dark chocolate chips (sugar free)
- ½ cup dried parsley
- 2 teaspoons vanilla extract
- 1 teaspoon peppermint extract
- A pinch of salt
- Stevia to taste

DIRECTIONS:

1. Melt together dark chocolate chips and coconut oil over a double boiler.

2. Add all the ingredients to a food processor and pulse until smooth.

3. Pour into round molds and freeze.

ADDITIONAL TIP

Add in some chopped dried cherries to make this even more festive

NUTRITION FACTS (PER SERVING)

Calories: 251   Fat: 25g   Protein: 3g   Total Carbohydrates: 7g   Dietary Fiber: 1g   Net Carbohydrates: 6g

CHEDDAR
CUPCAKE

Serves : 1   Preparation time : 5 minutes   Cooking time : 1 minutes   Freezing time : None

INGREDIENTS:

- 2 tablespoons shredded cheddar cheese
- 2 tablespoons grass-fed butter
- 3 tablespoons almond meal
- 1 tablespoons chopped green chilies
- ½ teaspoon baking powder
- ¼ teaspoon cayenne pepper
- 1 egg
- A pinch of salt

DIRECTIONS:

1. Whisk the egg until smooth. Add to a coffee mug.

2. Mix the cheese and softened butter. Add in the rest of the ingredients. Mix well.

3. Add to the egg and mix well.

4. Microwave for 1 minute or until a toothpick inserted in the center comes out clean.

5. Eat straight from the mug.

NUTRITION FACTS (PER SERVING)

Calories: 492   Fat: 49g   Protein: 18g   Total Carbohydrates: 6g   Dietary Fiber: 3g   Net Carbohydrates: 3g

SEED-FILLED BOMBS

Serves   : 12
Preparation time : 35 minutes
Cooking time   : None
Freezing time   : 1 hours

ADDITIONAL TIP
You can add any combination of seeds that you like. I like making a nice colorful mixture

INGREDIENTS:

- ⅔ cup coconut butter
- 2 ½ tablespoons coconut oil
- 2 tablespoons cacao powder
- 1 tablespoon hemp seeds
- 1 tablespoon flaxseeds
- 1 tablespoon chia seeds
- 1 tablespoon pumpkin seeds
- 1 teaspoon vanilla extract
- Stevia to taste

DIRECTIONS:

1. Melt coconut butter and coconut oil over a double boiler.

2. Combine all the ingredients and pour into molds.

3. Refrigerate until they are semi-set and doughy. Keep stored in the fridge for further use.

NUTRITION FACTS (PER SERVING)

Calories: 121   Fat: 11g   Protein: 2g   Total Carbohydrates: 4g   Dietary Fiber: 3g   Net Carbohydrates: 1g

NUTTY GINGER BOMBS

Serves : 12
Preparation time : 5 minutes
Cooking time : None
Freezing time : 2 hours

ADDITIONAL TIP
Fresh ginger works best but if you don't have access to it, you can also use ground ginger

INGREDIENTS:

- 4 ounces shredded coconut
- 2 ounces grass-fed butter
- 2 ounces coconut oil
- 1 tablespoon grated ginger
- 1 teaspoon ground cinnamon
- 1 teaspoon vanilla extract
- ½ tablespoon crushed roasted cashews
- Stevia to taste
- A pinch of salt

DIRECTIONS:

1. Soften the butter and coconut oil.
2. Combine all the ingredients.
3. Pour into molds and freeze.

NUTRITION FACTS (PER SERVING)

Calories: 79   Fat: 9g   Protein: 0g   Total Carbohydrates: 1g   Dietary Fiber: 0g   Net Carbohydrates: 1g

CUSTARD CUPS

Serves : 12   Preparation time : 5 minutes   Cooking time : None   Freezing time : 40 minutes

INGREDIENTS:

- ½ pound grass-fed butter
- 2 cups coconut milk
- ½ cup coconut oil
- ½ cup shredded coconut
- ¼ cup protein powder
  (any flavor of your preference)
- 2 tablespoons gelatin
- 1 ½ teaspoons vanilla extract
- 6 teaspoons xylitol
- 5 egg yolks
- Stevia to taste

DIRECTIONS:

1. Beat the egg yolks until smooth and creamy.

2. Melt together butter and coconut oil in a saucepan. Add coconut milk to the mixture.

3. Add gelatin and keep stirring until gelatin dissolves and the mixture begins to thicken a little.

4. Remove from heat and allow to cool. Stir in protein powder and vanilla extract.

5. Pour into bowls and sprinkle shredded coconut on top.

6. Chill before serving.

ADDITIONAL TIP
You can make varying flavors by using different flavored protein powders.

NUTRITION FACTS (PER SERVING)

Calories: 349   Fat: 37g   Protein: 2g   Total Carbohydrates: 5g   Dietary Fiber: 1g   Net Carbohydrates: 4g

NUTTY WHITE
CHOCOLATE TRUFFLES

Serves : 12
Preparation time : 5 minutes
Cooking time : None
Freezing time : 1-2 hours

ADDITIONAL TIP

Granulated Stevia is optional. You can also sprinkle with some cocoa powder or shredded coconut.

INGREDIENTS:

- ½ cup chopped roasted pecans
- 4 tablespoons cocoa butter
- 4 tablespoons coconut butter
- 4 tablespoons coconut oil
- 1 teaspoon scraped vanilla bean
- Granulated and liquid Stevia to taste
- A pinch of salt

DIRECTIONS:

1. Combine all the ingredients to form a batter.

2. Pour into a bread pan lined with parchment paper.

3. Freeze until set.

4. Cut into squares and sprinkle with some granulated Stevia.

NUTRITION FACTS (PER SERVING)

Calories: 92   Fat: 10g   Protein: 0g   Total Carbohydrates: 1g   Dietary Fiber: 0g   Net Carbohydrates: 1g

FLUFFY
FAT BOMBS

Serves : 12   Preparation time : 10 minutes   Cooking time : 6 minutes   Freezing time : 1 hour

INGREDIENTS:

- 2 cups heavy cream
- ⅔ cup sour cream
- 2 teaspoons ground cinnamon
- 1 teaspoon scraped vanilla bean
- ¼ teaspoon ground cardamom
- 4 egg yolks
- Stevia to taste

DIRECTIONS:

1. Whisk egg yolks in a glass bowl until smooth and creamy.

2. Place the bowl over a double boiler and add in rest of the ingredients.

3. Remove from heat and cool to room temperature.

4. Refrigerate for about an hour and then whisk.

5. Pour into molds and freeze.

ADDITIONAL TIP
You can also add in some cocoa powder.

NUTRITION FACTS (PER SERVING)

Calories: 363   Fat: 40g   Protein: 2g   Total Carbohydrates: 1g   Dietary Fiber: 0g   Net Carbohydrates: 1g

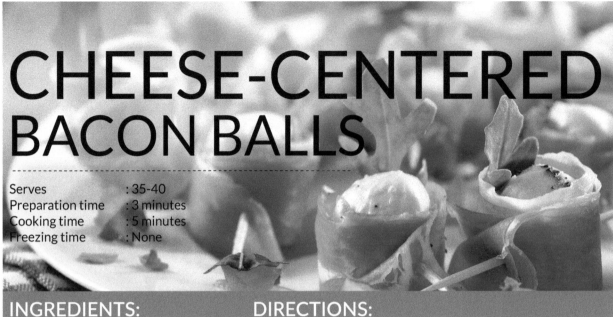

CHEESE-CENTERED
BACON BALLS

Serves : 35-40
Preparation time : 3 minutes
Cooking time : 5 minutes
Freezing time : None

INGREDIENTS:

- 35-40 slices bacon
- 16 ounces shredded mozzarella cheese
- 8 tablespoons grass-fed butter
- 8 tablespoons almond flour
- 6 tablespoons psyllium husk powder
- ¼ teaspoon onion powder
- ¼ teaspoon garlic powder
- 1 egg
- 2 cups clarified butter (or ghee or oil)
- Salt and pepper to taste

ADDITIONAL TIP

This does take a little bit of time as the wrapping process can be slow and tedious so plan ahead.

DIRECTIONS:

1. Prepare a double boiler.

2. Melt butter and add in half the mozzarella cheese. Wait for it to become gooey and sticky.

3. Add in the egg and beat with a fork until all is smooth.

4. Add in rest of the ingredients, minus the bacon and remaining cheese, and mix well. Remove from heat.

5. At this point it will have a thick, dough-like consistency. Allow to cool and then roll out into a flat triangular shape.

6. Spread the remaining cheese on half of the dough and then fold it over, like a sandwich with cheese in the middle.

7. Fold it over once more and seal the edges using your hands.

8. Cut into small squares, you'll get about 35-40.

9. Wrap a slice of bacon around each piece and secure with a toothpick. Repeat for all.

10. Heat oil/ghee in a deep pot and deep fry until brown and crispy.

11. Serve straight away.

NUTRITION FACTS (PER SERVING)

Calories: 275   Fat: 31g   Protein: 0g   Total Carbohydrates: 2g   Dietary Fiber: 1g   Net Carbohydrates: 1g

SPRING

GRASSHOPPER CHOCOLATE *Cups*

INGREDIENTS:

- 1 cup unsweetened dark chocolate chips
- 2 Tbsp. coconut oil
- 1 tsp. pure peppermint extract
- 10 drops liquid stevia
- ½ tsp. sea salt

Difficulty Level: 2 | 10 minutes (plus chilling time) | 2 minutes | x8 (1 cup each) $$

GF DF P

DIRECTIONS:

1. Add mini muffin tin liners to a baking sheet and set aside.
2. Make the chocolate coating by adding the coconut oil to a stockpot over low heat. Melt the oil and then add the chocolate chips and salt.
3. Stir the mixture continuously until completely melted.
4. Stir in the peppermint extract and stevia.
5. Pour the mixture into the mini muffin liners, filling about ¾ of the way.
6. Freeze for about 15 minutes or until set.
7. Store leftovers in the fridge or freezer.

Preparation Instructions:

You can replace the peppermint extract and use vanilla or almond extract instead if desired.

Serving Suggestions:

Serve with a cup of unsweetened almond milk.

Nutritional Information:

Carbs: 8g

Fiber: 4g

Net Carbs: 4g

Fat: 19g

Protein: 4g

Calories: 231

SAMOAS FAT *Bombs*

INGREDIENTS:

- 1 cup raw cashews
- 2 Tbsp. butter (use ghee for a paleo version)
- 2 Tbsp. unsweetened coconut butter
- 1 Tbsp. Swerve sweetener (use coconut sugar for a paleo option)
- 2 Tbsp. unsweetened coconut cream
- 1 tsp. pure vanilla extract
- 1 tsp. blackstrap molasses
- ½ tsp. sea salt
- ½ cup shredded unsweetened coconut

| Difficulty Level: 1 | 15 minutes (plus chilling time) | 0 minutes | x20 (1 fat bomb each) $$ |

GF

DIRECTIONS:

1. Line a baking sheet with parchment paper and add the shredded unsweetened coconut to a large bowl. Set aside.
2. Add the cashews, butter, and coconut butter to a high-speed blender or food processor, and process until the cashews are ground finely.
3. Add the Swerve, coconut cream, vanilla, molasses, and salt and blend again.
4. Form into 20 bite-sized rounds and roll into the shredded unsweetened coconut.
5. Place on the parchment lined baking sheet and set in the fridge for 30 minutes before enjoying.
6. Store leftovers covered in the fridge or the freezer.

Preparation Instructions:

If you are in a pinch, you can freeze the fat bombs for 15 minutes or refrigerate for 30 minutes.

Serving Suggestions:

Serve with a cup of coffee or tea.

Nutritional Information:

Carbs: 6g

Fiber: 1g

Net Carbs: 5g

Fat: 11g

Protein: 2g

Calories: 120

EASTER DAY CARROT CAKE FAT *Bombs*

Difficulty Level: 1	15 minutes (plus chilling time)	0 minutes	x14 (1 fat bomb per serving) $$

GF V P

INGREDIENTS:

- 1 cup walnuts
- 1 cup unsweetened coconut butter
- ½ cup shredded carrots
- ½ cup shredded unsweetened coconut
- 1 tsp. powdered stevia
- 1 tsp. pure vanilla extract
- 1 tsp. ground cinnamon
- ⅛ tsp. ground nutmeg
- ⅛ tsp. ground ginger

Preparation Instructions:

You can use pecans or cashews in place of the walnuts if preferred.

Serving Suggestions:

Serve with a cup of tea for a tasty Easter dessert treat.

DIRECTIONS:

1. Add walnuts, coconut butter, shredded carrots, and half of the shredded coconut to a food processor or high-speed blender and blend until combined well.
2. Add in the remaining ingredients minus the shredded coconut, and blend until combined.
3. Chill for 15 minutes in the fridge.
4. Roll into bite-sized rounds and roll into the remaining shredded unsweetened coconut.
5. Enjoy and store leftovers in the fridge or the freezer.

Nutritional Information:	
Carbs: 11g	**Fat:** 29g
Fiber: 6g	**Protein:** 5g
Net Carbs: 5g	**Calories:** 320

ALMOND BUTTER *Cups*

Difficulty Level: 2

20 minutes (plus chilling time)

3 minutes

x10 (1 almond butter cup each) $$

GF DF P

INGREDIENTS:

Chocolate Coating:
- 1 cup unsweetened dark chocolate chips
- 2 Tbsp. coconut oil
- ½ tsp. sea salt

Almond Butter Filling:
- ¼ cup unsweetened almond butter
- 1 tsp. powdered stevia
- 1 tsp. pure vanilla extract
- 1 Tbsp. coconut flour

Nutritional Information:

Carbs: 9g   **Fat:** 19g

Fiber: 4g   **Protein:** 4g

Net Carbs: 5g **Calories:** 230

DIRECTIONS:

1. Add mini muffin tin liners to a baking sheet and set aside.
2. Make the chocolate coating by adding the coconut oil to a stockpot over low heat. Melt the oil and then add the chocolate chips and salt.
3. Stir the mixture continuously until completely melted.
4. Once melted, scoop about 1 teaspoon of the chocolate mixture into the mini muffin liners to cover the bottom. Place in the freezer for about 15 minutes or until set.
5. While the chocolate is setting, make the almond butter filling by adding the almond butter, vanilla, and stevia to a mixing bowl and stir.
6. Add the coconut flour and mix well.
7. Once hardened, add about a teaspoon of the almond butter filling to the mini muffin liners and top with about 2 more teaspoons of the melted chocolate mixture.
8. Freeze for another 15-20 minutes or until hardened.
9. Store in the fridge or freezer until ready to enjoy.

LEMON COCONUT
Savory Bites

INGREDIENTS:

- 1 cup cream cheese
- 4 Tbsp. ghee, softened
- 10 drops liquid stevia
- 1 Tbsp. freshly squeezed lemon juice
- ½ cup shredded unsweetened coconut

Difficulty Level: 1 | 15 minutes (plus chilling time) | 0 minutes | x14 (1 bite per serving) $$

GF

DIRECTIONS:

1. Add cream cheese, ghee, and stevia to a high-speed blender or food processor and whip until the mixture is fluffy.
2. Add the lemon juice and whip again.
3. Scoop the mixture into silicone mini cupcake molds and sprinkle with the shredded coconut.
4. Freeze for about 1 hour before enjoying.
5. Store leftovers in the freezer.

Preparation Instructions:

You can use butter instead of ghee if preferred.

Serving Suggestions:

Serve with a dollop of whipped cream if desired.

Nutritional Information:

Carbs: 1g

Fiber: 0g

Net Carbs: 1g

Fat: 10g

Protein: 1g

Calories: 100

SAINT PATRICK'S DAY *Brownies*

Difficulty Level: 2	15 minutes	30-35 minutes	x8 (1 brownie per serving) $$

GF

INGREDIENTS:

- 2 cups almond flour
- 2 eggs
- 1 stick butter, melted (use coconut oil for a paleo version)
- ¼ cup raw unsweetened cocoa powder
- 1 tsp. pure peppermint extract
- 1 tsp. stevia powder
- 1 tsp. gluten- and aluminum-free baking powder
- ⅛ tsp. sea salt
- 2 Tbsp. water

Mint Frosting:

- 1 cup whipped cream cheese (use full-fat unsweetened coconut cream for a paleo version)
- 1 drop liquid stevia
- 1 tsp. plant-based green food coloring (artificial coloring-free)

DIRECTIONS:

1. Preheat the oven to 350 degrees F and line a 9x13-inch baking pan with parchment paper.
2. Add the eggs to a mixing bowl and whisk.
3. Mix in the butter, peppermint extract, and stevia. Mix well.
4. Add the almond flour, baking powder, sea salt, and water. Mix well.
5. Pour the mixture into the lined baking pan and bake for 30-35 minutes or until a toothpick inserted into the center comes out clean.
6. While the brownies are baking, make the peppermint frosting by adding the whipped cream cheese to a mixing bowl with the green food coloring, peppermint extract, and stevia. Using a handheld mixer, whip until a fluffy consistency forms.
7. Once the brownies are cooled, top with the frosting, and then slice into 8 squares.
8. Store leftovers in the fridge.

Preparation Instructions:

You can add ¼ cup of unsweetened dark chocolate chips to the batter for an added savory taste.

Serving Suggestions:

Serve with a mug of coffee or tea.

Nutritional Information:

Carbs: 5g	**Fat:** 17g
Fiber: 2g	**Protein:** 8g
Net Carbs: 3g	**Calories:** 192

FUNFETTI BIRTHDAY SHEET *Cake*

Difficulty Level: 3 | 20 minutes | 25-30 minutes | x18 (1 slice per serving) $$

GF

INGREDIENTS:

For Sprinkles:

- ½ cup shredded unsweetened coconut
- Assortment of plant-based food coloring colors

For Cake:

- 2 cups finely ground almond flour
- 2 eggs
- 2 cups whipped cream cheese
- ¼ cup unsweetened almond milk
- 1 stick butter, melted
- 1 tsp. pure vanilla extract
- ¼ cup Swerve
- 1 tsp. baking powder
- Coconut oil for greasing

For Whipped Cream:

- 2 cups heavy whipping cream
- 1 drop liquid stevia
- 1 tsp. pure vanilla extract

Preparation Instructions:

Feel free to use whatever low-calorie sweetener you prefer in the cake recipe.

Serving Suggestions:

Serve with a glass of unsweetened almond milk.

Nutritional Information:	
Carbs: 6g	**Fat:** 22g
Fiber: 1g	**Protein:** 4g
Net Carbs: 5g	**Calories:** 216

DIRECTIONS:

1. Preheat the oven to 350 degrees F and grease a large cake pan with coconut oil.
2. Make the funfetti sprinkles by dividing the shredded coconut into as many different bowls as you would like, depending on how many colors you choose to use. Use about 3-4 drops of food coloring per bowl and stir to coat the shredded coconut completely. Set aside.
3. Add the almond flour, Swerve, and baking powder to a bowl. Whisk to combine and then set aside.
4. In a separate bowl, add the eggs, melted butter, whipped cream cheese, vanilla, and almond milk and whisk well.
5. Pour the dry mixture into the egg mixture and stir until combined well.
6. Fold in the sprinkles and stir well.
7. Pour the mixture into the cake pan and bake for 25-30 minutes or until a toothpick inserted into the center comes out clean.
8. While the cake is baking, make the whipped cream by adding all the ingredients to a food processor and blend until a whipped cream-like consistency forms. Store in the fridge until ready to use.
9. Allow the cake to cool, and then serve with whipped cream immediately before serving.

SEA SALT VANILLA ALMOND BUTTER
Milkshake

Difficulty Level: 1	5 minutes	0 minutes	x2 (about ½ cup per serving) $$

GF DF P

DIRECTIONS:

1. Add all ingredients to a high-speed blender and blend until smooth.
2. Enjoy right away.

Preparation Instructions:

If you are not avoiding dairy, you can use ½ cup of heavy cream and 1 cup of whole milk in this recipe.

Serving Suggestions:

Serve with a dollop of unsweetened whipped cream if desired.

INGREDIENTS:

- 1 cup unsweetened almond milk
- 2 Tbsp. almond butter
- 1 tsp. pure vanilla extract
- 1 drop liquid vanilla cream stevia
- 1 pinch of sea salt

Nutritional Information:

Carbs: 4g	**Fat:** 11g
Fiber: 2g	**Protein:** 4g
Net Carbs: 2g	**Calories:** 124

RASPBERRY ICE CREAM *Sundae*

INGREDIENTS:

- 1 can unsweetened full-fat coconut cream
- ¼ cup frozen raspberries
- 1 tsp. pure vanilla extract
- 1 tsp. liquid stevia

Toppings:
- 4 Tbsp. sugar-free chocolate syrup
- ¼ cup walnut pieces

Difficulty Level: 1 | 10 minutes (plus chilling time) | 0 minutes | x8 $$

GF DF P

DIRECTIONS:

1. Add the coconut cream, raspberries, vanilla, and stevia to a high-speed blender, and blend until smooth.
2. Top with the sugar-free chocolate syrup and walnut pieces and serve.

Preparation Instructions:

You can use strawberries in place of raspberries if preferred.

Serving Suggestions:

Serve with a dollop of whipped cream if desired.

Nutritional Information:
Carbs: 6g
Fiber: 1g
Net Carbs: 5g
Fat: 15g
Protein: 3g
Calories: 170

STRAWBERRY MINT *Yogurt*

Difficulty Level: 1	10 minutes (plus chilling time)	0 minutes	x6 (approx. ⅓ cup serving each) $$

GF

INGREDIENTS:

- 2 cups full-fat unsweetened Greek yogurt (use full-fat unsweetened coconut milk yogurt for a paleo version)
- 1 cup strawberries
- 1 tsp. freshly chopped mint leaves
- 1 tsp. pure vanilla extract

DIRECTIONS:

1. Add all the ingredients to a high-speed blender, and blend until smooth.
2. Chill in the fridge for 1 hour before serving.
3. Enjoy, and store leftovers covered in the fridge.

Preparation Instructions:

You can use raspberries or blueberries in this recipe if preferred.

Serving Suggestions:

Serve with a dollop of whipped cream if desired.

Nutritional Information:

Carbs: 5g

Fiber: 1g

Net Carbs: 4g

Fat: 3g

Protein: 7g

Calories: 80

EASTER-INSPIRED COCONUT CREAM
Pie Pudding

Difficulty Level: 1	15 minutes (plus chilling time)	0 minutes	x6 (approx. ½ cup per serving) $$

GF

INGREDIENTS:

- 2 cups full-fat unsweetened coconut milk
- 1 cup heavy cream (use another 1 cup of full-fat unsweetened coconut milk for a paleo version)
- 2 Tbsp. ghee, melted
- ½ cup erythritol
- 1 cup shredded unsweetened coconut, divided
- 1 tsp. pure vanilla extract

DIRECTIONS:

1. Add the coconut milk, heavy cream, vanilla, and melted ghee to a food processor, and blend until smooth.
2. Add the erythritol and ½ cup of shredded coconut.
3. Chill for 1 hour.
4. Once chilled, divide among 6 cups and top with additional shredded coconut and serve.

Preparation Instructions:

Feel free to use 1 drop of liquid stevia in place of the erythritol if preferred.

Serving Suggestions:

Serve with a dollop of whipped cream if desired.

Nutritional Information:

Carbs: 7g

Fiber: 3g

Net Carbs: 4g

Fat: 35g

Protein: 3g

Calories: 340

KEY LIME PIE *Pudding*

INGREDIENTS:

- 1 cup full-fat unsweetened coconut milk
- 2 Tbsp. sour cream (use coconut cream for a paleo version)
- 1 Tbsp. erythritol (use pure maple syrup for a paleo version)
- ¼ cup freshly squeezed lime juice
- 1 tsp. pure vanilla extract
- ½ cup shredded unsweetened coconut
- 1 cup of walnuts, processed into crumbs

| Difficulty Level: 1 | 15 minutes (plus chilling time) | 0 minutes | x6 $$ |

GF

DIRECTIONS:

1. Start by adding the walnuts to a food processor and blend just until crumbled. Set aside.
2. Add all ingredients minus the shredded unsweetened coconut to a blender or food processor and blend until creamy.
3. Split the crumbled walnuts to the bottom of 6 serving bowls and then evenly divide the key lime mixture among the bowls.
4. Top with shredded coconut.
5. Chill for 30 minutes before serving.

Preparation Instructions:

You can use cream cheese in place of sour cream if preferred.

Serving Suggestions:

Serve with a dollop of whipped cream if desired.

Nutritional Information:

Carbs: 8g

Fiber: 3g

Net Carbs: 5g

Fat: 25g

Protein: 6g

Calories: 255

PISTACHIO BROWNIE BATTER *Milkshake*

Difficulty Level: 1 | 5 minutes | 0 minutes | x2 $$

GF

INGREDIENTS:

- ½ cup heavy cream (use coconut milk for a paleo version)
- ½ cup unsweetened almond milk
- 3 drops liquid stevia
- 2 Tbsp. raw unsweetened cocoa powder
- 1 Tbsp. raw cocoa nibs
- 2 Tbsp. roasted unsalted pistachios

DIRECTIONS:

1. Add all ingredients to a high-speed blender and blend until smooth.
2. Serve right away.

Preparation Instructions:

You can use any low-carb sweetener of choice.

Serving Suggestions:

Serve with a dollop of whipped cream if desired.

Nutritional Information:

Carbs: 6g

Fiber: 3g

Net Carbs: 3g

Fat: 16g

Protein: 3g

Calories: 165

RED VALENTINES

Serves	: 12
Preparation time	: 5 minutes
Cooking time	: None
Freezing time	: 2 hours

ADDITIONAL TIP

If you don't have a piping bag or don't know how to operate one, then just get a flexible ice tray. Scoop the mixture into the ice compartments and freeze. You can get cute shapes for extra fun.

INGREDIENTS:

- 2 ounces half and half
- 4 diced strawberries
- 4 pitted cherries
- 4 tablespoons coconut oil
- 4 tablespoons grass-fed butter
- Stevia to taste

DIRECTIONS:

1. Add the diced strawberries and the cherries to a high-speed food processor. Pulse until pureed.

2. Add the half and half and Stevia. Blend so that everything is mixed well.

3. Melt the butter over a double boiler or in the microwave and add to the mixture. Also add the coconut oil and mix well.

4. Add the mixture to a piping bag. Squeeze out little droplets onto a baking tray and freeze for a few hours.

5. Keep stored in the freezer and enjoy as needed.

NUTRITION FACTS (PER SERVING)

Calories: 78   Fat: 9g   Protein: 0g   Total Carbohydrates: 1g   Dietary Fiber: 0g   Net Carbohydrates: 0g

CHOCOLATE
COCONUT BOMBS

Serves : 12
Preparation time : 20 minutes
Cooking time : None
Freezing time : 1 hour

ADDITIONAL TIP
You can also add in about ½ cup shredded coconut for some texture.

INGREDIENTS:

- 1 cup coconut oil (solid)
- ½ cup dark cocoa powder
- 1 teaspoon peppermint extract
- ½ teaspoon vanilla extract
- 5 drops Stevia
- A pinch of salt

DIRECTIONS:

1. Add all the ingredients to a food processor and blend until combined.

2. Use a teaspoon to drop spoonfuls onto parchment paper.

3. Refrigerate until solidified and keep refrigerated.

NUTRITION FACTS (PER SERVING)

Calories: 126   Fat: 14g   Protein: 0g   Total Carbohydrates: 0g   Dietary Fiber: 0g   Net Carbohydrates: 0g

PEANUT BUTTER EXPLOSION

Serves   :12
Preparation time   :10 minutes
Cooking time   :None
Refrigeration time :30 minutes

ADDITIONAL TIP

You can also use almond butter or hazelnut butter instead of peanut butter.

INGREDIENTS:

- ¼ cup creamy, unsweetened peanut butter
- 2 Tbsp. grass-fed butter or ghee
- 1 Tbsp. coconut oil
- 2-3 drops of stevia
- ½ cup shredded unsweetened coconut
- 1 cup of sifted coconut flour
- ¼ tsp. salt
- ½ cup crushed peanuts

DIRECTIONS:

1. Start by adding the peanut butter, butter or ghee, coconut oil, and stevia to a stockpot over low/medium heat and whisk until melted.

2. Add in the unsweetened coconut, coconut flour, and salt. Stir to combine.

3. Transfer the mixture to a bowl and place in the fridge covered for 30 minutes.

4. While the mixture is chilling, add the crushed peanuts to a mixing bowl and set aside.

5. Once the mixture chilled, roll into balls and then roll into the crushed peanuts.

6. Store leftovers covered in the fridge.

NUTRITION FACTS (PER SERVING)

Calories: 93   Fat: 9g   Protein: 2g   Carbohydrates: 3g   Net Carbohydrates: 2g   Fiber: 1g

CREAM CHEESE CRATERS

Serves   : 12
Preparation time : 5 minutes
Cooking time   : None
Freezing time   : 3 hours

ADDITIONAL TIP

You can also use mascarpone cheese instead of cream cheese.

INGREDIENTS:

- ½ cup full-fat cream cheese
- ½ cup chopped walnuts or nuts of choice
- ½ cup grated dark chocolate
- Stevia to taste

FOR THE FILLING:

- 4 tablespoons grass-fed butter
- 2 tablespoons espresso powder
- 2 tablespoons heavy cream
- Stevia to taste

DIRECTIONS:

1. Soften the cream cheese and mix in the dark chocolate, chopped nuts and Stevia.

2. Take 12 mini cupcake liners and line the sides with the mixture so as to make a crater shape.

3. Place in the freezer for about 2 hours.

4. Meanwhile, melt the butter and whip in the heavy cream. Fold in rest of the filling ingredients.

5. Take the craters out of the freezer and fill each one with a small amount of filling.

6. Store in the refrigerator and enjoy whenever you like.

NUTRITION FACTS (PER SERVING)

Calories: 100   Fat: 10g   Protein: 2g   Total Carbohydrates: 2g   Dietary Fiber: 0g   Net Carbohydrates: 2g

SAVORY
SALMON BITES

Serves : 12   Preparation time : 5 minutes   Cooking time : None   Freezing time : None

INGREDIENTS:

- 50g smoked salmon trimmings
- 1 cup mascarpone cheese
- ⅔ cup grass-fed butter (softened)
- 1 tablespoon apple cider vinegar
- 1 tablespoon chopped parsley
- Salt to taste

DIRECTIONS:

1. Soften the cheese using a fork and mix in the vinegar, parsley and salt.

2. Add the butter and salmon trimmings and mix well.

3. Form into small balls and line on parchment paper.

4. Refrigerate until firm.

ADDITIONAL TIP

Try mackerel instead of salmon for a different taste.

NUTRITION FACTS (PER SERVING)

Calories: 117   Fat: 13g   Protein: 3g   Total Carbohydrates: 1g   Dietary Fiber: 0g   Net Carbohydrates: 1g

COCONUT
CHOCOLATE FUDGE

Serves   : 12
Preparation time : 10 minutes
Cooking time   : None
Freezing time   : Overnight

ADDITIONAL TIP

Add in some chopped nuts for a nutty flavor.

INGREDIENTS:

- ⅓ cup dark chocolate chips
- ½ cup cocoa powder
- ½ cup coconut oil
- ¼ cup full-fat coconut milk
- 1 teaspoon vanilla extract
- Stevia to taste

DIRECTIONS:

1. Melt the coconut oil and add to a blender.

2. Add in the rest of the ingredients and blend until smooth and creamy.

3. Line a bread pan with parchment paper and pour in the mixture.

4. Freeze overnight.

5. Cut into small squares and store in the refrigerator.

NUTRITION FACTS (PER SERVING)

Calories: 78   Fat: 8g   Protein: 1g   Total Carbohydrates: 4g   Dietary Fiber: 1g   Net Carbohydrates: 3g

MATCHA
& DARK CHOCOLATE CUPS

Serves : 12   Preparation time : 10 minutes   Cooking time : None   Freezing time : 2 hours

INGREDIENTS:

- 10 ounces dark chocolate chips
- ¼ cup grass-fed butter
- ½ tablespoon matcha green tea powder
- 2 teaspoons coconut oil
- Stevia to taste

DIRECTIONS:

1. Melt the chocolate chips over a double boiler and stir in the coconut oil.

2. Grease or line a muffin tray and brush the chocolate mixture onto the sides.

3. Transfer to a freezer for about an hour.

4. Meanwhile, soften the butter and mix in the matcha powder and Stevia.

5. When the crusts of the cups are set, remove from the freezer and scoop in the matcha mixture.

6. Store in the refrigerator and use as needed.

ADDITIONAL TIP
You can add more matcha powder if you want a stronger flavor.

NUTRITION FACTS (PER SERVING)

Calories: 135   Fat: 14g   Protein: 1g   Total Carbohydrates: 3g   Dietary Fiber: 2g   Net Carbohydrates: 1g

LIMEY SAVORY PIE

Serves : 12
Preparation time : 5 minutes
Cooking time : 7 minutes
Freezing time : 2 hours

ADDITIONAL TIP

I personally like a cheeky drizzle of melted dark chocolate on top. It complements the lime well.

INGREDIENTS:

- 1 cup almond flour
- 3 tablespoons butter
- 1 tablespoon ground cinnamon
- ½ teaspoon vanilla extract
- Stevia to taste

FOR THE FILLING:

- 4 ounces full-fat cream cheese
- ¼ cup coconut oil
- 3 tablespoons grass-fed butter
- 2 limes
- Stevia to taste
- A handful of baby spinach (optional – adds color)

DIRECTIONS:

1. Mix the first five ingredients to form a crumble mixture.

2. Press this mixture into the bottom of 12 muffin cups and bake for 7 minutes at 350 degrees.

3. While the crusts are baking, juice the lime and grate for zest.

4. Add all the filling ingredients to a food processor and blend until smooth.

5. Cool the crusts to room temperature and then pour this mixture in the center. Freeze until set.

NUTRITION FACTS (PER SERVING)

Calories: 146   Fat: 15g   Protein: 3g   Total Carbohydrates: 2g   Dietary Fiber: 1g   Net Carbohydrates: 1g

ST. PATRICK'S SCRUMPTIOUS FUDGE

Serves : 12
Preparation time : 10 minutes
Cooking time : None
Freezing time : Overnight

ADDITIONAL TIP

1. Use shamrock-shaped molds for a fun presentation.
2. Include some ground nuts for a different taste.

INGREDIENTS:

- 10 ounces coconut oil
- 4 tablespoons cocoa powder
- 2 tablespoons granulated Stevia
- ½ teaspoon peppermint extract

DIRECTIONS:

1. Combine all the ingredients and mix well.
2. Pour into molds or ice trays and refrigerate overnight.
3. Voila! Easy and delicious fat bombs are ready.

NUTRITION FACTS (PER SERVING)

Calories: 206   Fat: 24g   Protein: 0g   Total Carbohydrates: 0g   Dietary Fiber: 0g   Net Carbohydrates: 0g

FENNEL
& ALMOND BITES

Serves : 12   Preparation time : 5 minutes   Cooking time : None   Freezing time : 3 hours

INGREDIENTS:

- ¼ cup almond milk
- ¼ cup almond oil
- ¼ cup cacao powder
- 1 teaspoon fennel seeds
- 1 teaspoon vanilla extract (optional)
- A pinch of salt

DIRECTIONS:

1. Mix the almond milk and almond oil and beat until smooth and glossy. Use an electric beater for quicker results.

2. Mix in rest of the ingredients.

3. Pour into a piping bag and get creative with the shapes. Make sure to use parchment paper as a base or they might stick.

4. Freeze for 3 hours and then keep stored in the refrigerator.

ADDITIONAL TIP
You can also use coconut milk and coconut oil instead of almond.

NUTRITION FACTS (PER SERVING)

Calories: 172   Fat: 20g   Protein: 1g   Total Carbohydrates: 1g   Dietary Fiber: 1g   Net Carbohydrates: 0g

WHITE
CHOCOLATE BOMBS

Serves   : 12
Preparation time : 15 minutes
Cooking time   : 5 minutes
Freezing time   : 1 hour

ADDITIONAL TIP

Try different types of chocolate to create a great variety of bombs!

INGREDIENTS:

- 4 ounces cocoa butter
- 1 ½ cups chopped pecans or walnuts
- 6 tablespoons grass-fed butter
- 6 tablespoons coconut oil
- ¾ teaspoon vanilla extract
- ⅛ teaspoon sea salt
- Stevia to taste

CHOCOLATE COATING:

- ¼ ounce cocoa butter
- 1 ounce white baking chocolate, unsweetened
- ⅛ teaspoon stevia extract
- ⅛ teaspoon vanilla extract

DIRECTIONS:

1. Melt the butter, cocoa powder and coconut oil over a double boiler. Mix well.

2. Add in the rest of the (non-chocolate coating) ingredients and combine.

3. Pour into your favorite molds/cupcake pan and place in the refrigerator overnight.

4. To prepare the white chocolate coating, melt the chocolate and butter over a double broiler and add in the vanilla and stevia.

5. Remove the base from the molds and dip in the chocolate coating. Then leave in the fridge for 2-3 hours to set.

NUTRITION FACTS (PER SERVING)

Calories: 287   Fat: 30g   Protein: 1g   Total Carbohydrates: Less than 1g   Dietary Fiber: 0g
Net Carbohydrates: Less than 1g

CREAMY
AVOCADO & BACON BALLS

Serves : 12   Preparation time : 10 minutes   Cooking time : 15 minutes   Freezing time : None

INGREDIENTS:

- 1 avocado
- 1 chili pepper
- 1 onion
- ½ cup grass-fed butter
- 4 bacon slices
- 1 tablespoon fresh lime juice
- ¼ teaspoon sea salt
- A pinch of pepper

DIRECTIONS:

1. Chop the onions and chili peppers (deseed if you prefer it a bit milder).
2. Fry the bacon in its grease until crispy.
3. Cut and dice the avocado.
4. Add all the ingredients, including the bacon grease (not the bacon itself), to a food processor and blend until smooth.
5. Chop the bacon and mix with the creamy mixture.
6. Drop spoonfuls onto parchment paper.
7. Refrigerate for 2-3 hours.
8. Serve when firm.

ADDITIONAL TIP

If you are not a fan of spicy food, either use a mild chili pepper or leave it out altogether.

NUTRITION FACTS (PER SERVING)

Calories: 156   Fat: 15g   Protein: 3g   Total Carbohydrates: 3g   Dietary Fiber: 1g   Net Carbohydrates: 1g

MACAROONS

Serves : 12   Preparation time : 10 minutes   Cooking time : 15 minutes   Freezing time : None

INGREDIENTS:

- ½ cup coconut flakes
- ¼ cup almond meal
- 1 tablespoon coconut oil
- 1 teaspoon vanilla extract
- 3 egg whites
- Stevia to taste

DIRECTIONS:

1. Sift together all the dry ingredients.
2. Melt coconut oil and stir in the vanilla extract.
3. Pour the coconut oil into the dry mixture and mix well.
4. Beat the egg whites until stiff peaks form.
5. Fold into the other mixture.
6. Drop spoonfuls onto a baking tray lined with parchment paper.
7. Bake for 8 minutes at 400 degrees.
8. Cool and enjoy!

ADDITIONAL TIP

If you have trouble getting the egg whites to form stiff peaks, use a chilled bowl and lots of patience.

NUTRITION FACTS (PER SERVING)

Calories: 46   Fat: 5g   Protein: 2g   Total Carbohydrates: Less than 1g   Dietary Fiber: 0g
Net Carbohydrates: Less than 1g

FROZEN COOKIE DOUGH *Fat Bombs*

INGREDIENTS:

- 1 cup raw cashews
- ½ cup coconut butter
- 1 tsp. pure vanilla extract
- 10 drops liquid vanilla stevia
- ¼ tsp. sea salt
- 4 Tbsp. unsweetened dark chocolate chips

Difficulty Level: 1	10 minutes (plus chilling time)	0 minutes	x14 (1 fat bomb per serving) $$

GF DF P

DIRECTIONS:

1. Add raw cashews and coconut butter to a food processor or high-speed blender and blend until the cashews are ground finely.
2. Add the vanilla, stevia, and salt and blend until combined.
3. Fold in the dark chocolate chips.
4. Freeze for 20 minutes and then roll into bite-sized rounds.
5. Store in the fridge or freezer until ready to enjoy.

Preparation Instructions:

You can use raw cocoa nibs in place of the dark chocolate chips is preferred.

Serving Suggestions:

Top each fat bomb with a dollop of unsweetened whipped cream if desired.

Nutritional Information:

Carbs: 9g

Fiber: 4g

Net Carbs: 5g

Fat: 19g

Protein: 3g

Calories: 206

FROZEN SUPER CHUNK BROWNIE *Fat Bombs*

Difficulty Level: 1 | 10 minutes (plus chilling time) | 0 minutes | x14 (1 fat bomb per serving) $$

GF **DF** **P**

INGREDIENTS:

- 1 cup raw almonds
- 2 Tbsp. raw unsweetened cocoa powder
- ½ cup coconut butter
- 1 tsp. pure vanilla extract
- 10 drops liquid vanilla stevia
- ¼ tsp. sea salt
- 4 Tbsp. unsweetened dark chocolate chips

Preparation Instructions:

You can use raw cocoa nibs in place of the dark chocolate chips is preferred.

Serving Suggestions:

Top each fat bomb with a dollop of unsweetened whipped cream if desired.

DIRECTIONS:

1. Add raw almonds and coconut butter to a food processor or high-speed blender and blend until the almonds are ground finely.
2. Add the vanilla, stevia, and salt and blend until combined.
3. Fold in the dark chocolate chips.
4. Freeze for 20 minutes and then roll into bite-sized rounds.
5. Store in the fridge or freezer until ready to enjoy.

Nutritional Information:

Carbs: 8g	**Fat:** 18g
Fiber: 5g	**Protein:** 3g
Net Carbs: 3g	**Calories:** 191

STRAWBERRY
Mousse

Difficulty Level: 1 | 10 minutes (plus chilling time) | 0 minutes | x4 (approx. ½ cup per serving) $$

GF

INGREDIENTS:

- 1 cup full-fat unsweetened coconut milk
- 1 cup heavy cream
- ½ cup frozen strawberries
- 1 tsp. pure vanilla extract
- 2 tsp. Swerve
- 1 Tbsp. freshly squeezed lemon juice

DIRECTIONS:

1. Add all the ingredients to a blender or food processor, and blend until creamy.
2. Divide among 4 bowls and chill for 1 hour before serving.
3. Chill for 30 minutes before serving.

Preparation Instructions:

You can use an additional 1 cup of coconut milk in place of the heavy cream if you are avoiding dairy.

Serving Suggestions:

Serve with unsweetened shredded coconut if desired.

Nutritional Information:

Carbs: 5g

Fiber: 0g

Net Carbs: 5g

Fat: 15g

Protein: 1g

Calories: 148

SUPER CREAMY CHOCOLATE PEANUT BUTTER *Milkshake*

INGREDIENTS:

- ½ cup unsweetened almond milk
- ¼ cup coconut milk
- 1 Tbsp. raw cacao powder
- 2 Tbsp. peanut butter
- 3 drops liquid stevia
- 1 tsp. pure vanilla extract

Difficulty Level: 1 | 5 minutes | 0 minutes | x2 (about ½ cup per serving) $$

GF DF

DIRECTIONS:

1. Add all ingredients to a high-speed blender, and blend until smooth.
2. Serve right away.

Preparation Instructions:

If you are not avoiding dairy, you can use ½ cup of heavy cream and 1 cup of whole milk in this recipe.

Serving Suggestions:

Serve with a dollop of unsweetened whipped cream if desired.

Nutritional Information:

Carbs: 7g

Fiber: 3g

Net Carbs: 4g

Fat: 16g

Protein: 5g

Calories: 185

DECADENT BLACKBERRY
Ice Cream (NO CHURN)

INGREDIENTS:

- 1 cup heavy cream
- 1 cup sour cream
- ½ cup frozen blackberries
- 10 drops liquid vanilla stevia

DIRECTIONS:

1. Add all ingredients to a high-speed blender, and blend until smooth.
2. Pour into a large plastic container and freeze for about 4 hours or until solid.
3. Let sit at room temperature for a few minutes before serving.

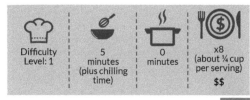

Difficulty Level: 1	5 minutes (plus chilling time)	0 minutes	x8 (about ¼ cup per serving) $$

GF

Preparation Instructions:

Feel free to use any berry of choice in this recipe.

Serving Suggestions:

Serve with a dollop of unsweetened whipped cream if desired.

Nutritional Information:

Carbs: 3g	**Fat:** 12g
Fiber: 1g	**Protein:** 1g
Net Carbs: 2g	**Calories:** 117

RASPBERRIES & CREAM
Ice Cream (NO CHURN)

INGREDIENTS:

- 1 cup heavy cream
- 1 cup whipped cream cheese
- ½ cup frozen raspberries
- 10 drops liquid vanilla stevia
- 1 tsp. pure vanilla extract

DIRECTIONS:

1. Add all ingredients to a high-speed blender, and blend until smooth.
2. Pour into a large plastic container and freeze for about 4 hours or until solid.
3. Let sit at room temperature for a few minutes before serving.

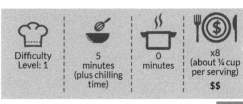

Difficulty Level: 1	5 minutes (plus chilling time)	0 minutes	x8 (about ¼ cup per serving) $$

GF

Preparation Instructions:

Feel free to use any berries of choice in this recipe.

Serving Suggestions:

Serve with a dollop of unsweetened whipped cream if desired.

Nutritional Information:

Carbs: 5g	Fat: 16g
Fiber: 1g	Protein: 3g
Net Carbs: 4g	Calories: 171

VEGAN BLUEBERRY FROZEN *"Yogurt"*

INGREDIENTS:

- 2 cans unsweetened coconut cream
- ½ cup frozen blueberries
- 10 drops liquid vanilla stevia
- 1 tsp. pure vanilla extract

Difficulty Level: 1 | 5 minutes (plus chilling time) | 0 minutes | x8 $$

GF DF P

DIRECTIONS:

1. Add all ingredients to a high-speed blender, and blend until smooth.
2. Pour into a large plastic container and freeze for about 4 hours or until solid.
3. Let sit at room temperature for a few minutes before serving.

Preparation Instructions:

Feel free to use any berries of choice in this recipe.

Serving Suggestions:

Serve with a dollop of unsweetened whipped cream if desired.

Nutritional Information:

Carbs: 4g

Fiber: 1g

Net Carbs: 3g

Fat: 26g

Protein: 3g

Calories: 255

STRAWBERRIES & CREAM FROZEN
"Yogurt" Popsicles

INGREDIENTS:

- 1 cup heavy cream
- 1 cup sour cream
- ½ cup frozen strawberries
- 10 drops liquid vanilla stevia

GF

DIRECTIONS:

1. Add all ingredients to a high-speed blender, and blend until smooth.
2. Pour into 6 Popsicle molds and freeze for 4-6 hours or until completely hardened before serving.

Preparation Instructions:

Feel free to use any berries of choice in this recipe.

Serving Suggestions:

You can dunk the top of the Popsicles into melted unsweetened dark chocolate and set in the freezer for 10 minutes for an even more decadent treat.

Nutritional Information:

Carbs: 3g

Fiber: 0g

Net Carbs: 3g

Fat: 15g

Protein: 2g

Calories: 155

ORANGE *Creamsicles*

Difficulty Level: 1 | 5 minutes (plus chilling time) | 0 minutes | x6 (1 popsicle per serving) $

GF

INGREDIENTS:

- 1 cup heavy cream (use full-fat unsweetened coconut milk for a paleo version)
- ½ cup unsweetened almond milk
- ¼ cup freshly squeezed orange juice
- 10 drops liquid vanilla stevia

DIRECTIONS:

1. Add all ingredients to a high-speed blender, and blend until smooth.
2. Pour into 6 Popsicle molds and freeze for 4-6 hours or until completely hardened before serving.

Preparation Instructions:

You can use coconut milk in place of the heavy cream for a dairy-free version.

Serving Suggestions:

Drizzle the Popsicle with unsweetened chocolate syrup if desired.

Nutritional Information:

Carbs: 2g

Fiber: 0g

Net Carbs: 2g

Fat: 8g

Protein: 1g

Calories: 77

SAVORY MOCHA *Milkshake*

| Difficulty Level: 1 | 5 minutes | 0 minutes | x2 (approx. ½ cup per serving) $ |

GF

INGREDIENTS:

- 1 cup heavy cream
- 2 Tbsp. butter, melted
- ½ cup brewed coffee, chilled
- 1 Tbsp. unsweetened almond butter
- 1 Tbsp. raw cocoa nibs
- 1 handful of ice

- **Optional Toppings:** Whipped cream and no sugar added chocolate syrup

Preparation Instructions:

Use coconut milk in place of the heavy cream and eliminate the butter for a dairy-free version.

Serving Suggestions:

Serve with a dollop of unsweetened whipped cream.

DIRECTIONS:

1. Add all ingredients to a high-speed blender, and blend until smooth.
2. Pour into glasses and serve.
3. If using, top with whipped cream and no sugar added chocolate syrup.

Nutritional Information:

Carbs: 5g	**Fat:** 41g
Fiber: 1g	**Protein:** 3g
Net Carbs: 4g	**Calories:** 390

COCONUT CHOCOLATE
Chip Popsicles

Difficulty Level: 1	10 minutes (plus chilling time)	0 minutes	x8 (1 popsicle per serving) $$

GF DF P

INGREDIENTS:

- 2 cups full-fat unsweetened coconut milk
- ½ cup coconut butter
- 1 tsp. pure vanilla extract
- ¼ cup chopped walnuts
- 10 drops liquid stevia
- 4 Tbsp. unsweetened dark chocolate chips

DIRECTIONS:

1. Add coconut milk, coconut butter, vanilla, walnuts, and stevia to a high-speed blender or food processor. Blend to combine.
2. Fold in the chocolate chips.
3. Pour into Popsicle molds and freeze for 4-6 hours or until completely solid before serving.

Preparation Instructions:

You can use any nut butter of choice in this recipe.

Serving Suggestions:

Drizzle the Popsicles with unsweetened chocolate syrup if desired.

Nutritional Information:

Carbs: 11g

Fiber: 6g

Net Carbs: 5g

Fat: 30g

Protein: 4g

Calories: 311

CHOCOLATE & ALMOND
Mint Pudding

Difficulty Level: 1 | 10 minutes (plus chilling time) | 0 minutes | x4 $$

GF **DF** **P**

INGREDIENTS:

- 2 very ripe avocados, pitted and peeled
- ¼ cup full-fat unsweetened coconut milk
- ¼ cup raw unsweetened cocoa powder
- ½ tsp. almond extract
- ¼ tsp. pure peppermint extract
- 10 drops liquid stevia
- ⅛ tsp. sea salt

DIRECTIONS:

1. Add all the ingredients to a blender or food processor, and blend until creamy.
2. Chill for 30 minutes before enjoying.
3. Once chilled, enjoy right away.

Preparation Instructions:

You can use heavy cream in place of the coconut milk if not avoiding dairy.

Serving Suggestions:

Serve with chopped almonds if desired.

Nutritional Information:

Carbs: 13g

Fiber: 9g

Net Carbs: 4g

Fat: 24g

Protein: 3g

Calories: 253

HOMEMADE STRAWBERRY WHIPPED
Cream Parfait

INGREDIENTS:

- 1 cup heavy whipping cream
- 1 tsp. pure vanilla extract
- 10 drops of liquid vanilla stevia
- 1 cup strawberries, halved

Difficulty Level: 2 | 20 minutes | 0 minutes | x4 (approx. ¼ cup per serving) $$

GF

DIRECTIONS:

1. Make whipped cream by adding the heavy whipping cream to a large bowl with the vanilla extract and stevia.
2. Whip using a handheld mixer until stiff peaks form.
3. Add half of the strawberries to the base of a glass jar or large bowl and top with half of the whipped cream.
4. Repeat these 2 layers.
5. Divide into 4 servings and serve.

Preparation Instructions:

You can use full-fat unsweetened coconut milk for a dairy-free version.

Serving Suggestions:

Serve with freshly chopped mint leaves for added flavor.

Nutritional Information:

Carbs: 4g

Fiber: 1g

Net Carbs: 3g

Fat: 11g

Protein: 1g

Calories: 118

TANGY COCO BOMBS

Serves : 12
Preparation time : 5 minutes
Cooking time : None
Freezing time : 3 hours

ADDITIONAL TIP

If the cream cheese separates during mixing (might happen due to the tartness of limes), don't worry. Your fat bombs will still turn out awesome.

INGREDIENTS:

- 2 ounces full-fat cream cheese
- ½ ounce coconut flakes
- ¼ cup grass-fed butter
- ½ cup coconut oil
- 2 tablespoons coconut cream
- 2 teaspoons vanilla extract
- 2 limes
- Stevia to taste

DIRECTIONS:

1. Juice the limes and grate for zest.

2. Melt together the butter and coconut oil.

3. Remove from heat and mix in the coconut cream and cream cheese. Mix well.

4. Add in the rest of the ingredients (except the coconut flakes) and mix well.

5. Roll into small balls and roll in the coconut flakes so they receive a good coating.

6. Place into either molds or cupcake pan and freeze.

NUTRITION FACTS (PER SERVING)

Calories: 122   Fat: 14g   Protein: 1g   Total Carbohydrates: 1g   Dietary Fiber: 0g   Net Carbohydrates: 1g

MASCARPONE
MOCHA FAT BOMBS

Serves	: 12
Preparation time	: 10 minutes
Cooking time	: None
Freezing time	: 3 hours

ADDITIONAL TIP

You can also mix by hand but it will take much longer.

INGREDIENTS:

- ½ cup mascarpone cheese
- 3 tablespoons granulated Stevia
- 2 tablespoons grass-fed butter
- 1 tablespoon coconut oil
- 1 ½ tablespoon cacao powder, divided
- ½ teaspoon rum (optional)
- ¼ teaspoon instant coffee
- More Stevia to taste

DIRECTIONS:

1. Add all the ingredients (reserve ½ tablespoon cacao powder) to a blender and pulse until consistency is smooth and creamy.

2. Pour into silicone molds and sprinkle the remaining cacao powder on top.

3. Freeze and enjoy.

NUTRITION FACTS (PER SERVING)

Calories: 77   Fat: 8g   Protein: 1g   Total Carbohydrates: 1g   Dietary Fiber: 0g   Net Carbohydrates: 1g

TROPICAL TRUFFLES

Serves : 12
Preparation time : 45 minutes
Cooking time : None
Freezing time : 2 hours

ADDITIONAL TIP

You can also coat with cocoa powder instead of chopped nuts.

INGREDIENTS:

- ⅔ cup protein powder (any flavor)
- ¼ cup coconut milk
- ¼ cup white chocolate chips
- 4 tablespoons coconut flakes
- 4 tablespoons coconut oil

FOR THE TOPPING:

- ⅔ cup coconut butter
- 3 tablespoons chopped nuts
- 1 teaspoon coconut oil

DIRECTIONS:

1. Mix the non-topping ingredients until it is thoroughly combined and pour into molds. Freeze until the base is set. This will typically take an hour.

2. Meanwhile, melt together the coconut butter and coconut oil.

3. Dip each frozen truffle in the mixture and sprinkle with chopped nuts.

4. Return to the freezer for another half an hour (or store in the fridge) and enjoy!

NUTRITION FACTS (PER SERVING)

Calories: 249   Fat: 26g   Protein: 5g   Total Carbohydrates: 2g   Dietary Fiber: 1g   Net Carbohydrates: 1g

PEPPERONI
PIZZA PASTRIES

Serves : 12   Preparation time : 20 minutes   Cooking time : None   Freezing time : None

INGREDIENTS:

- 14 beef pepperoni slices
- 8 button mushrooms
- 8 pitted olives
- 4 ounces mascarpone cheese
- 2 tablespoons pesto
- 2 tablespoons chopped basil
- Salt and pepper to taste

DIRECTIONS:

1. Slice the pepperoni, olives and mushrooms into small pieces.

2. Sauté the mushrooms in a pan for 2-3 minutes, until brown. Then allow to cool.

3. In a bowl, combine the cheese, pesto, salt and pepper.

4. Add the olives, mushrooms, pepperoni and basil. Mix well.

5. Form into small balls and serve. No need to freeze or cook.

ADDITIONAL TIP
Get creative and add as many toppings as you like.

NUTRITION FACTS (PER SERVING)

Calories: 110   Fat: 11g   Protein: 2g   Total Carbohydrates: 2g   Dietary Fiber: 0g   Net Carbohydrates: 2g

CHIVES & CHEESE

Serves : 12
Preparation time : 5 minutes
Cooking time : None
Freezing time : None

ADDITIONAL TIP
Stack together with cherry tomatoes to make a great starter

INGREDIENTS:

- 2 ½ ounces full-fat cream cheese
- ¼ cup fresh chives
- Salt to taste
- Almond flour

DIRECTIONS:

1. Thinly chop the chives.

2. Soften the cream cheese and mix it together with the chives and salt. Add almond flour to adjust the consistency.

3. Form into small balls and chill for about 30 minutes in the refrigerator.

NUTRITION FACTS (PER SERVING)

Calories: 38   Fat: 3g   Protein: 7g   Total Carbohydrates: Less than 1g   Dietary Fiber: 0g
Net Carbohydrates: Less than 1g

JELL-O
FAT BOMBS

Serves : 12   Preparation time : 10 minutes   Cooking time : None   Freezing time : 2 hours

INGREDIENTS:

- 8 ounces full-fat cream cheese
- 1 pack Jell-O (any flavor and sugar-free)
- 1 teaspoon lemon juice

DIRECTIONS:

1. Soften the cream cheese and mix in the lemon juice.
2. Form into small balls.
3. Roll in Jell-O and place in the fridge overnight.

ADDITIONAL TIP

Add some chopped fruit of the same flavor as the Jell-O for extra fruity goodness.

NUTRITION FACTS (PER SERVING)

Calories: 105   Fat: 9g   Protein: 3g   Total Carbohydrates: 1g   Dietary Fiber: 0g   Net Carbohydrates: 1g

BERRY CHEESE NUT BALLS

Serves	: 12
Preparation time	: 10 minutes
Cooking time	: None
Freezing time	: None

ADDITIONAL TIP

Drizzle a little olive oil on top a softer flavor

INGREDIENTS:

- 6 ounces goat cheese
- ⅔ cup dried cranberries
- ¼ cup chopped pecans
- 2 tablespoons chopped parsley
- Salt to taste

DIRECTIONS:

- Chop the cranberries into small pieces.
- Soften the cheese and mix together all the ingredients.
- Form into small balls and chill for about 45 minutes
- Serve and enjoy!

NUTRITION FACTS (PER SERVING)

Calories: 125   Fat: 10g   Protein: 7g   Total Carbohydrates: 3g   Dietary Fiber: 1g   Net Carbohydrates: 2g

MINI
STRAWBERRY CHEESECAKES

Serves : 12   Preparation time : 10 minutes   Cooking time : None   Freezing time : 2-3 hours

INGREDIENTS:

- 1 cup coconut butter
- 1 cup coconut oil
- ½ cup sliced strawberries
- 2 tablespoons full-fat cream cheese
- ½ teaspoon lime juice
- Stevia to taste

DIRECTIONS:

1. Add the strawberries to a food processor and puree.

2. Soften the cream cheese and coconut butter.

3. Combine all the ingredients.

4. Add to silicone molds and freeze for about 2 hours. Keep stored in the refrigerator.

ADDITIONAL TIP
try raspberries or blackberries instead of strawberries.

NUTRITION FACTS (PER SERVING)

Calories: 372   Fat: 41g   Protein: 1g   Total Carbohydrates: 3g   Dietary Fiber: 1g   Net Carbohydrates: 2g

ICE CREAM
FAT BOMBS

Serves : 12   Preparation time : 10 minutes   Cooking time : None   Freezing time : 2 hours

INGREDIENTS:

- 3 cups protein powder of your favorite ice cream flavor
- 1 cup cashew butter
- 1 cup whipped cream
- Stevia to taste

DIRECTIONS:

1. Place the whipped cream in a bowl and gently fold in protein powder, Stevia, and cashew butter.

2. Pour the mixture in silicone molds and freeze.

3. Enjoy the frozen dessert.

ADDITIONAL TIP
Top with some chopped berries or sugar-free syrup

NUTRITION FACTS (PER SERVING)

Calories: 250   Fat: 19g   Protein: 11g   Total Carbohydrates: 10g   Dietary Fiber: 2g   Net Carbohydrates: 8g

BLUEBERRY BOMBS

Serves : 12
Preparation time : 15 minutes
Cooking time : None
Freezing time : 3-4 hours

ADDITIONAL TIP

The berries do not have to be blue-try your favorite berries instead.

INGREDIENTS:

- 2 tablespoons almond butter
- 1 tablespoon coconut oil
- 1 tablespoon cacao powder
- ¼ teaspoon ground cinnamon
- Stevia to taste
- A pinch of salt

FOR THE TOPPING:

- ¼ cup grass-fed butter
- ¼ cup cream cheese
- ¼ cup pureed blueberries
- 1 tablespoon heavy whipping creams
- 1 teaspoon vanilla extract

DIRECTIONS:

1. Combine the non-topping ingredients in a bowl to form an even mixture.

2. Spread in a bread pan lined with parchment paper. Freeze until set.

3. In the meantime, add the topping ingredients to a blender and whirl to whip them up.

4. Remove the base from freezer and cut into squares. Spread the topping on each square and return to the freezer.

NUTRITION FACTS (PER SERVING)

Calories: 77   Fat: 8g   Protein: 1g   Total Carbohydrates: 1g   Dietary Fiber: 0g   Net Carbohydrates: 1g

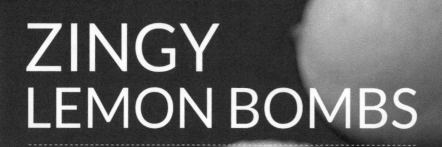

ZINGY
LEMON BOMBS

Serves : 12
Preparation time : 5 minutes
Cooking time : None
Freezing time : 2 hours

ADDITIONAL TIP

You can also pop them onto sticks like lollipops. All you have to do is stick a wooden skewer into each mold

INGREDIENTS:

- 4 ounces cream cheese
- ¼ cup grass-fed butter
- ¼ cup coconut oil
- 3-4 lemons
- Stevia to taste
- Yellow food coloring (optional)

DIRECTIONS:

1. Juice the lemons and grate for zest.

2. Add all the ingredients to a food processor and mix well.

3. Pour into molds and freeze until set.

NUTRITION FACTS (PER SERVING)

Calories: 75   Fat: 8g   Protein: 2g   Total Carbohydrates: 1g   Dietary Fiber: 0g   Net Carbohydrates: 1g

TINY SPICY EXPLOSIONS

Serves : 12   Preparation time : 25 minutes   Cooking time : None   Freezing time : None

INGREDIENTS:

- 12 ounces cream cheese
- 3 jalapeno peppers
- 12 bacon slices
- 1 ½ teaspoons dried parsley
- ¾ teaspoon garlic powder
- ¾ teaspoon onion powder
- ¼ teaspoon kosher salt
- Pepper to taste

DIRECTIONS:

1. Fry the bacon until crispy and chop into tiny pieces.
2. Slice the jalapeno peppers thinly.
3. Soften the cream cheese and combine all the ingredients (including bacon and jalapenos).
4. Form into small balls and chill for about 30 minutes.
5. Serve with a dip of choice.

ADDITIONAL TIP

Don't waste the bacon grease. Add it to the mix as well.

NUTRITION FACTS (PER SERVING)

Calories: 207   Fat: 19g   Protein: 5g   Total Carbohydrates: 2g   Dietary Fiber: 1g   Net Carbohydrates: 1g

CHEESY GARLIC FAT BOMBS

Serves	: 12
Preparation time	: 7-10 minutes
Cooking time	: None
Freezing time	: None

ADDITIONAL TIP

You can also add in some chopped vegetables if you like.

INGREDIENTS:

- 4 cups shredded mozzarella cheese
- 1 cup keto crumbs
- 4 tablespoons grass-fed butter
- 2 teaspoons garlic paste
- 2 teaspoons cilantro paste
- Salt to taste

DIRECTIONS:

1. Mix all the ingredients. The consistency will be dough-like.

2. Using your hands, make into small irregular shapes. It will be difficult to get them to form balls.

3. Roll in keto crumbs and lay on parchment paper.

4. Refrigerate until firm (about 1-2 hours).

5. Serve with a dip of choice.

NUTRITION FACTS (PER SERVING)

Calories: 141   Fat: 11g   Protein: 9g   Total Carbohydrates: 1g   Dietary Fiber: 0g   Net Carbohydrates: 1g

Copyright 2019 by Elizabeth Jane - All rights reserved.

ISBN 978-0-9975842-5-7

For permissions contact:

elizabeth@ketojane.com or visit http://ketojane.com/

This document is geared towards providing exact and reliable information in regards to the topic and issue covered. The publication is sold with the idea that the publisher is not required to render professional advice, officially permitted, or otherwise, qualified services. If advice is necessary, legal or professional, a practiced individual in the profession should be ordered.

From a Declaration of Principles which was accepted and approved equally by a Committee of the American Bar Association and a Committee of Publishers and Associations.

In no way is it legal to reproduce, duplicate, or transmit any part of this document in either electronic means or printed format. Recording of this publication is strictly prohibited, and any storage of this document is not allowed unless with written permission from the publisher. All rights reserved.

The information provided herein is stated to be truthful and consistent, in that any liability, in terms of inattention or otherwise, by any usage or abuse of any policies, processes, or directions contained within is the sole and utter responsibility of the recipient reader. Under no circumstances will any legal responsibility or blame be held against the publisher for any reparation, damages, or monetary loss due to the information herein, either directly or indirectly.

The information herein is off ered for informational purposes solely and is universal as so. The presentation of the information is without contract or any type of guarantee assurance.

The author is not a licensed practitioner, physician or medical professional and off ers no medical treatments, diagnoses, suggestions or counseling. The information presented herein has not been evaluated by the United States Food and Drug Administration, and it is not intended to diagnose, treat, cure or prevent any disease. Full medical clearance from a licensed physician should be obtained before beginning or modifying any diet, exercise or lifestyle program, and physicians should be informed of all nutritional changes.

The author claims no responsibility to any person or entity for any liability, loss or damage caused or alleged to be caused directly or indirectly as a result of the use, application or interpretation of the information presented herein.

CPSIA information can be obtained
at www.ICGtesting.com
Printed in the USA
LVHW071105160920
666167LV00005B/42